Inhibitions in Work and Love

Psychoanalytic Approaches to Problems in Creativity

Inhibitions in Work and Love
Psychoanalytic Approaches to Problems in Creativity

Herbert S. Strean
Editor

The Haworth Press
New York

Inhibitions in Work and Love: Psychoanalytic Approaches to Problems in Creativity has also been published as *Current Issues in Psychoanalytic Practice,* Volume 1, Number 1, Spring 1984.

The Haworth Press, Inc., 28 East 22 Street, New York, NY 10010

Library of Congress Cataloging in Publication Data
Main entry under title:

Inhibitions in work and love.

   ''Has also been published as Current issues in psychoanalytic practice, vol. 1, number 1, spring 1984''—T.p. verso.
   Includes bibliographies.
   1. Creative ability—Addresses, essays, lectures. 2. Inhibition—Addresses, essays, lectures. I. Strean, Herbert S.
BF408.I52   1984   153.3'5   83-22757
ISBN 0-86656-276-1

Inhibitions in Work and Love

Current Issues in Psychoanalytic Practice
Volume 1, Number 1

CONTENTS

A LETTER FROM THE EDITOR

Dear Reader:

Welcome to *Current Issues in Psychoanalytic Practice.* The Editorial Board of this journal is very hopeful that this issue and future ones will stimulate and enrich your own work with patients and your own clinical repertoire.

With so many journals on the market, you might ask, "What makes *Current Issues in Psychoanalytic Practice* unique? The query deserves an answer. We of the Society for Psychoanalytic Training and The New York Center for Psychoanalytic Training have felt for some time that what is lacking in the professional literature are scholarly papers which focus sharply on therapist-patient interactions and most particularly which focus on the therapist's activities. We are dedicating ourselves to providing you with a journal that will attempt to bring you into the consulting room so that you can become keenly aware of how your colleagues deal with transference and countertransference issues, how they attempt to resolve resistances, and how they try to make the unconscious become conscious.

This journal will be a topical journal in that each issue will be devoted to a particular theme that deeply concerns mental health professionals. The current issue on inhibitions in creativity is one that concerns all of us. Aren't most practitioners trying to liberate creativity in all of their patients? Doesn't so much of our work involve our striving to help our patients better understand those blocks which interfere with their expression of mature creativity? We are quite confident that this issue will help you and your patients be more creative individuals.

We expect to turn out four issues of this journal per year. Number two of this year's series will deal with problems of violence and hatred, and later issues will focus on difficult patients and on sexuality.

1

We will welcome receiving papers on all of the above-mentioned topics from mental health professionals and from members of allied professional disciplines. We are particularly interested in essays that focus on practice and will favor those papers that emanate from the perspective of mainstream psychoanalysis, i.e., where the unconscious of the patient is highly respected and related to with rigor and where transference, countertransference and working with resistances are all part of the clinician's professional *modus vivendi*.

Dear Reader, we will be pleased to receive suggestions and comments—critical and non-critical—we look forward to your sending articles to us, and we hope that you will enjoy *Current Issues in Psychoanalytic Practice* for many years to come.

Cordially,

Herbert S. Strean
Editor

The Effect of Psychoanalysis on the Creative Individual

Reuben Fine

From the very beginning psychoanalysis was intimately involved with the creative process. At an early stage Freud saw the connection between analysis and creativity, though he held on to the erroneous belief that the artist is somehow halfway between the normal and the neurotic (Freud, 1908). But he also observed (1904) that in such an artistic production as a play the author and the audience both vary within fairly well-defined limits: only a certain type of neurotic, e.g. can enjoy certain types of art, such as gruesome murder scenes. Freud was also friendly personally with a large number of artists, particularly writers; Jones mentions the Zweigs, Arnold and Stefan, Thomas Mann, Gerhardt Hauptmann, and H.G. Wells, among others.

At the same time creative individuals have always been strongly drawn to analysis, and many have gone through the process, either for personal problems or for the sake of increasing their productivity. In the early days e.g. the most renowned advocate of the cultural benefits of analysis was Thomas Mann, then regarded as the world's leading creative writer.

Yet we still know all too little of the effect of psychoanalysis on the creative personality. There is the well-worn belief that somehow analyis will rob the artist of his gifts; while this has no real foundation in fact, it remains widely held, and prevents many creative individuals from entering analysis. My purpose in this paper is to put together what we do know as well as possible, and to see what conclusions can be reasonably drawn. Of course, the effects of psychoanalysis in general are hard to measure and hard to evaluate, so its specific application to the creative individual introduces even more complications, but the effort to integrate what is known is well worthwhile.

THE EDRITA FRIED STUDY

In 1964 Edrita Fried and a number of collaborators published a book *Artistic Productivity and Mental Health* which bears directly on some of the questions considered here. The study was based on the therapeutic results with six artists; a sculptor, three painters, one actor-singer and a writer. The therapy was three times a week analytic psychotherapy, and the attempt was made to evaluate the relationship between changes in personality and changes in the artists' work habits. Each artist was observed and data were collected for at least three years. The subjects were all persons who had achieved a considerable degree of artistic expression and technical skill.

In an introduction the well-known sculptor Chaim Gross expressed some interesting opinions. He felt that the artist has to be happy in his personal life and have peace of mind so that he can create. "I feel that if you have a good spouse half your work is done."[1] The artist has to be an honest person. Organization and a certain amount of order are conditions for working well as an artist. He stresses that talent is necessary; if talent is missing, the psychoanalytic treatment will not provide it.[2] With bona fide artists he notes that they have often benefited a lot from treatment. "Treatment can sometimes open a person's vision."

One interesting comment is that real artists do not suffer from work blocks. "I, myself, work long hours from morning to evening, and when I get home I relax a bit. I am ready again to start sketching. I don't consider myself the exception but rather the rule."[3] In another paper (Fine, 1980) I have made a similar comment about creativity, work and depression: creativity is the capacity to work, depression is the inability to work. Gross' optimistic remark about the absence of work blocks among real artists would not be shared by others; rather the opposite, even the greatest of artists have demonstrated serious work blocks. Leonardo e.g. took years to finish his paintings, and at one time almost abandoned art (Freud, 1910). Picasso, in spite of his extraordinary productivity, also had many periods in which he could do little or nothing (Gedo, 1982). The work block is in fact the most common symptom that brings artists to psychoanalysis.

The summary provided at the end of the Fried book makes the following points. The productivity of the artists was not hindered by the therapy; quite the opposite; both with regard to quantity of output and with regard to the constructiveness and appropriateness of the work patterns which were studied in detail there was positive development. As a matter of fact, she says, the improvements obtained were even more marked than the study shows. The research funds covered only three years. Actually, nearly all the artists remained in therapy beyond the observation period, financing the therapy themselves. In all cases substantial further gains were made during these subsequent, privately-financed periods.

In the majority of cases the ratings describing the forward movement in work patterns were higher than those describing the forward movement as far as development of the total personality is concerned. Another way of putting this is that any changes in psychic balance, in the defense structure, in identification, self-esteem, etc. were first reflected in the work patterns.

E.g. several artist patients complained of a state of being bogged down in ritual to the point where spontaneity was scarce, primarily because in inhibiting aggressive and sexual impulses that were sensed as dangerous the individual inhibited the entire emotional life. All of the artists suffered in varying degrees from lack of spontaneity and the concurring rigidity. E.g. one whom they call Matthew Taylor, reported the existence of a hairline balance between drive and control, a constant battle between explosive ideas and the immediate compulsive need for extinction of the idea. This see-saw alternation between drive and defense was represented graphically in an oppressive preoccupation with symmetry. In the course of his analysis this preoccupation with symmetry disappeared entirely, thus effecting a near-total change in his work.

In all cases a variety of work problems and personality difficulties sprang from powerfully stored quantities of aggression which were inhibited, sometimes projected upon others, and at times covered up by reaction formations in the form of politeness, helpfulness and general pleasantness. Only when the controls were lifted and the artists became both more aware of their aggression and also more able to express aggression and opposition, did work difficulties in the form of lethargy, tightness or depression disappear.

With only one exception, the artist patients all had grandiose ideas concerning their talents and products. Having produced notable works that had found acclaim, they had their eyes fixed on ever more outstanding artistic successes. Invariably, such ambitions led to an intensification of narcissistic expectations. Nearly all the artists destroyed too many works before and in the early phases of treatment because they were intent on producing masterpieces and felt, often in retrospect wrongly, that created pieces did not measure up to omnipotent expectations. In the course of treatment this grandiose narcissism was reduced to reasonable proportions in varying degrees. (It may be noted incidentally that this is a conflict which affects all artists and is handled by them outside analysis in varying ways.)

As to the relationships with other human beings, all the artists improved. Nor did this in any way detract from their ability to settle down to creative work. Quite the contrary. As they got along better, more energy was freed to pursue creative work. One highly important observation that she makes is that most of the artists whom they observed and treated were inordinately passive when they entered treatment. This passivity gave way to greater activity and assertion. In every case where passivity gave way to activity work patterns were affected positively. Although she does not say so this passivity must obviously have been related to the grandiose narcissism which was so prominent.

In all cases connections between specific personality problems and work pattern flaws were noted, and often corrected. No further generalizations are ventured here.

Thus in sum, the therapy of these six artists improved their work capacity, helped them to overcome blocks, led to more gratifying interpersonal relationships and led to a better life all around. They all moved in the direction of the analytic ideal, though in varying degrees.

What should be emphasized also is that no new talent was created here—what was done was the removal of blocks to the release of abilities which were there all along. This too must be woven into our theory.

WHAT IS CREATIVITY?

Definitions of creativity are legion. I do not intend to offer a new one here, but rather to point out how inadequate much of the literature, both psychoanalytic and non-analytic, is. In the first place it has long been known that the sublimations of pure art and pure science are essentially the same (Sharpe, 1935). Thus in the study of creativity examples can be chosen from either science or art.

Second, many of the summary statements about creativity, including Freud's, may make good headlines but bear little relationship to psychological reality. The creative person is not necessarily either a genius or a madman (Niederland, 1976), the roots of creativity arc both in the id and in the ego, to pinpoint them all in the id, as was done in the early days of psychoanalysis (Freud), is to make a serious mistake; it is not a Janus-faced ability to seek two sides of a perception or ideal (Rothenberg, 1976); it is not a magic synthesis per se (Arieti, 1976), although it may be at times; it is not divergent productions per se (Guilford, 1967) although again it may be. One could go on and on, with the theories of creativity.

In essence, the creative person is someone who does something novel, either to himself or to others. If it is to himself, I call it inner creativity; if it is to others, I call it outer creativity. Almost all the literature deals with outer creativity, thus making the serious mistake of ignoring the inner world of the persons who were the creators. It is here that psychoanalysis historically made its greatest contributions, showing graphically what a close connection there can be between the personality and the object created; yet there is also something novel and unique, which has nothing to do with the personality as such.

Perhaps John Keats knew best when he described the process of artistic creation as the "innumerable compositions—and decompositions which take place between the intellect and its thousand materials before it arrives at that trembling, delicate and snail-born perception of beauty." (Quoted in Bychowski, 1951.)

If we cannot define creativity with any degree of precision, that implies that it is equally difficult to pinpoint what a creative person is. Here a useless argument so often intercedes: painter so-and-so does excellent work, but is he "creative?" The same for writers, actors, mathematicians and so on. Looked at carefully, the concept of "creativity" sought here has a truly mystical quality. For purposes of discussion and clarification let us define the creative individual as any one who produces in any one of the creative fields, including art and science. How *good or inspired* his acts of creation may be is a separate question. As we saw, in Freud's subjects, they all thought that they were really geniuses, and we know that this narcissistic grandiosity is a general characteristic of human beings, differing only in degrees. Thus if these two questions are separated we can reach more clarity.

Before we move on to a direct discussion of psychoanalysis (including analytic and other therapy) and the creative individual, we have to try to see what happens to the creative person outside analysis. As Freud once said, the only real control that can decide whether an analysis was successful or not, is to let the person live his life over again without analysis.

On this score we are overwhelmed with material. As we know many have claimed that creativity and madness are close. "We poets in our youth begin in gladness; But thereof comes in the end despondency and madness" (Wordsworth). Certainly some creative individuals have become mad, and this is especially noteworthy in the case of those who have done extraordinary work (cf. Newton) but that could scarcely be maintained as a definite generalization. Others are hacks; still others create one work of art and fade from the scene. In other words, creative individuals run the gamut of human personalities; the only thing that really distinguishes them from the common run of mankind is a certain talent which allows them to create.

Apart from clinical material, which must often be disguised, most of the illustrative material on creativity necessarily comes from well-known writers or artists. Can we then assume that those who are less gifted had the same kinds of struggles, or were they just less gifted? The answer again defies a facile generalization; creative persons simply run the gamut of human psychology. If we cite well-known persons, that is unavoidable, but it also must not be made to seem representative. In each case the relationship between the creative product and the individual's life must be carefully scrutinized.

Another factor that must be considered is the role of the surrounding culture. Creativity needs a certain environment, which has been called a creativogenic environment, in which to flourish (Ammons, 1962). "Full many a flower is born to blush unseen" and were it not for his remarkable poem "Elegy in a Country Churchyard," Thomas Gray would probably be completely unknown today. On the other hand, the system of art critics, book review editors and the rest often push mediocrities to heights of great achievement, and overlook many others. We tend to forget the old saying that those who can do, those who can't criticize.

While no overall statements are feasible, the lives of some of the leading artists of the present century may be reviewed to see what they were like, and to ask, in general, what might have happened to them had they been psychoanalyzed.

F. Scott Fitzgerald (1896-1940) has become known as the spokesman for the Jazz Age of the 1920's. He has also become a symbol for the successful writer who squanders his earnings, takes to drink, goes downhill and dies prematurely.

Fitzgerald hoped to be a writer from the time that he was in grade school. His first story appeared in print in the school magazine in 1909, when he was only 13 years old. Following the image of the writer in American fantasy he paid little attention to school, reading voraciously whatever he could.

After a few minor acceptances he reaped his first great success with *This Side of Paradise.* Then came the exciting adventurous life of an American expatriate in France. Fame and fortune were his. In 1925 came his greatest success, *The Great Gatsby,* still one of the most revealing pictures of that age.

After *Gatsby* and other minor successes the ride downhill began around 1930. His wife Zelda had a breakdown, and remained hospitalized the rest of her life. He began to drink heavily, which likewise lasted all his life.

The paradox of Fitzgerald's life is that he was more of an image in the eyes of the public than a successful writer. During his lifetime even his best novels never did too well, and he was always in debt. His royalties in 1939 were $33. When he died in 1940 he left $700 in cash, of which $613 went to the undertaker.[4]

As his biographer Le Vot notes, it was the man more than the novelist who made the headlines. After WWII a great enthusiasm developed for him, far more than anything he had ever experienced in his lifetime.

Whatever his literary status, Fitzgerald was a miserably unhappy man. In the spring of 1920, when he had just published a successful novel and married Zelda, he wrote:[5]

> Riding in a taxi one afternoon between very tall buildings under a mauve and rosy sky, I began to bawl because I had everything I wanted and knew I would never be so happy again.

At that time he was only 24. As he grew older the depression deepened. An autobiographical story called "Crack-Up" chronicled his personal disaster. At one point he says: "Of course all life is a process of breaking down."[6] In 1935 he wrote a letter to Mary Gingrich:[7] "As to health, the body has been gradually sliding toward annihilation for two years . . . I was doing my stuff on gin, cigarettes, bromides and hope."

Thus Fitzgerald's success overshadowed his private horror. As a man, he was depressed, a lifelong alcoholic, full of work difficulties, rarely reaching his best. Without realizing what was going on, he could let a sadistic Hemingway write to him:[8]

> If you really feel blue enough, get yourself heavily insured and I'll see that you can get killed . . . and I'll write you a fine obituary . . . and we can take your liver out and give it to the Princeton Museum, your heart to the Plaza Hotel, and one lung to Max Perkins and the other to George Horace Lorimer.

Although psychoanalysis was still a rarity in Fitzgerald's heydey, it was by no means unknown. What would have happened to him if he had been analyzed? Interestingly, he touches upon the subject in *Tender Is the Night* (1934). The hero Dick Diver, a psychiatrist, makes the mistake of falling in love with Nicole, a rich patient. He transfers his vitality to her. She gets better, takes him to America, where he goes steadily downhill, until she finally throws him out. Translated into the language of therapy, he was afraid of his hostility to the therapist, which would lead him to turn the therapist into a great man, then drag him down to despair, cynicism, disillusion and failure. A common enough theme in our analytic practice—the patient who wants to take the analyst's place and ruin him—but it was in Fitzgerald's unconscious. In a sense this also looms as a resistance to therapy in many artists—they become more interested in the fight against the analyst than in their own improvement. To answer our question: had Fitzgerald been analyzed in 1932, instead of writing *Tender Is the Night,* he could only have gone uphill, not slid further into the alcoholic depression that ended his life. Incidentally, after *Tender Is the Night* his creativity also came to an end, and he spent the last few years of his life as a hack writer for Hollywood.

A different picture emerges from the life of August Strindberg (1849-1912), the great Swedish writer who exerted such a powerful influence on modern literature, especially drama. Strindberg was one of the most prolific writers that have ever lived, his collected works running to some 55 volumes. His works are heavily autobiographical; a number of them (such as his early one *Maidservant's Son)* are direct autobiographies. During his life he had a number of breakdowns most of which he again described in various direct and indirect ways. His last play *The Great Highway* tried to reconcile the struggle within him between heaven and earth; it could not catch other people, and closed after one performance.

Strindberg was quite paranoid, eccentric, extremely rebellious, somewhat insane (in the popular sense of the word) and obviously a man struggling with terrible inner torment. All of this was handled by his writing, which seems to have gone on incessantly; with so much produced it is hard to see how he had time for anything else. But he did delve in alchemy, and accused the doctor who was treating him for his insanity of trying to steal his secret formula for gold-making.[9]

Had Strindberg been analyzed, what would have happened? Probably very little to his enormous literary productivity. But undoubtedly it would have made him a much happier person. He, too, was a lifelong alcoholic and depressive. But again, his paranoid reaction to his therapist (noted above, even though he was not an analyst) is noteworthy: his self-image as Sweden's greatest writer was far more important to him than achieving more mental health, even though he himself realized what terrible inner tortures he went through in his life.

A particularly interesting work for the topic of this paper is that of Eileen Simpson, *Poets in Their Youth* (1982). Mrs. Simpson was married to the poet John Berryman from 1942 to 1956; later she became a practicing psychotherapist. In the course of her life with Berryman (who later committed suicide) she knew intimately many of the well-known poets who were dominant in the U.S. after WWII, such as Berryman himself, R.P. Blackmur, Randall Jarrell, Robert Lowell and Delmore Schwartz. There was also some contact with older poets like T.S. Eliot and Ezra Pound.

All of these men, except for T.S. Eliot, had extraordinarily serious emotional problems. Berryman and Jarrell both suicided (though there is some question about Jarrell); Lowell was in and out of mental hospitals all of his life; Schwartz was seriously paranoid (he is a character in one of Saul Bellow's novels and is reported to have sued Bellow). Of Blackmur, whose wife committed suicide, Mrs. Simpson says that his wife would comment: "Richard won't admit it but what he wants in a wife is a mother."[10] Pound, as is well known, was a hospitalized schizophrenic at St. Elizabeth's in Washington for thirteen years. Once Berryman had consented to edit Pound's poems, Pound began to bombard him with notes, letters, telegrams and other communications which were largely unintelligible. (Pound will also appear later on in this paper in connection with Hilda Doolittle, who was analyzed by Freud.)

Although the details of the therapy of these men are scanty, the fact is that almost all seem to have had some kind. They were all conspicuously creative personalities. What was the effect of the therapy on them and their creativity? On the whole virtually none (though since too little is known, one cannot be sure. Berryman did commit suicide long after he broke up with Eileen, but his therapy might have forestalled an earlier suicide attempt).

Berryman is best known from her book, understandably. He was madly in love with her. If she didn't declare unconditional love for him immediately and soon, he was going to lose his mind—he would talk about how old he was and how little he had accomplished. Twenty-six and all he had to his name was a fifth of a book. For him the only thing was to write poetry. All else was a waste of time. At another point he said: ''What the hell is happiness? Should a poet seek it?''[11]

After years of nerve-wracking experiences (his famous book *The Dream Songs* was first entitled *The Nervous Songs*), Eileen finally induced John to seek out a psychiatrist. He responded with a poem:[12]

> Analysands all, and the rest ought to be
> The friends my innocence cherished, and you and I
> Darling—the friends I qualm and cherish to see.

This manic reaction did not lead to a good course of therapy. Eventually it seems to have petered out, until he became a severe alcoholic. Even then again he turned it into a poem:[13]

> O all the problems other people face
> We have intensified and could not face
> Until at last we feel completely alone
> Thick in a quart of company a day.

In similar vein Delmore Schwartz once commented that his analyst, a woman, was very bright, but ''How can I make a transference to an ugly woman?''[14]

So far as one can see, the therapy did not affect the artistic productivity of anyone in this group, one way or another. Nor did the therapy have any great effect or even value for them (though here the details are too skimpy).

We come up here against one of the major resistances to therapy of every artist. He is convinced that his art form is the only thing that is worthwhile, whether it happens to be music, poetry, plays, painting or anything else. He feels threatened that this obsession (for such it is) will be analyzed and thus taken away from him, although it could just as well be strengthened (as will be seen). As a result he fights the efforts of the analyst to try to understand his deepest preoccupations. When that happens the analysis proceeds against strong resistance. When it does not, which is also often the case, the resistance is minor; in fact, as the Fried study showed, artists in general make good analytic subjects.

Summing up, the artist often dooms himself to an unhappy life for the sake of his art. Many, as has often been seen, are great artists but miserable people (Matson, 1980). It is against such a background that the effectiveness of the psychoanalysis of the creative individual must be evaluated.

I wish to consider some clinical material now. This can be divided into four groups: those who are creative before analysis, those who give up their creative outlet during analysis, those who develop their creative ability during analysis, and those to whom creativity is a matter of no great interest.

FREUD'S CASES

A number of cases of Freud's in which he treated creative individuals have been preserved. As usual, they are worthy of study.

There is first of all the case of Freud himself. Here some comments about the history of psychoanalysis are in order (cf. Fine, 1979). Freud's intellectual odyssey is marked principally by his self-analysis, the first successful one in history. This was unknown for a long time, until the letters to Fliess were discovered and published after WWII. But they alone are not sufficient. Jones' short chapter on the self-analysis in his biography of Freud is likewise inadequate.

No one in history has been examined more closely than Freud. The French analyst Didier Anzieu has put together all the information, from others and from Freud's own work (such as *The Interpretation of Dreams* and the *Psychopathology of Everyday Life*), to reconstruct Freud's emotional journey from 1895 (when the self-analysis began) to 1902, when information becomes more public. Up to that time the main source of knowledge about Freud's inner life comes from his dreams, which are largely placed in chronological order by Anzieu and from Freud's occasional reminiscences. Anzieu's work is a masterpiece; it is unfortunate that it has not yet been translated into English (Anzieu, 1975).

The self-analysis changed Freud in many ways; it also changed the entire history of psychoanalysis. Anzieu by a careful comparison has shown that the number of concepts used by Freud in 1902 was about double the number used in 1895, before his self-analysis began. Furthermore, all of the main analytic concepts (as distinguished from the purely psychiatric which were common currency at that time) came out of the self-analysis: meaning of dreams, unconscious actions ("Freudian slips"), infantile sexuality, the primal scene, castration anxiety, autoeroticism, psychic trauma due to wish it evokes and so on. Thus his self-analysis led to the really original discoveries of psychoanalysis. This momentous event has been lost sight of in the course of history, because analysts have moved either to denigrate Freud or to idealize him. Both have involved ignoring the self-analysis.

What Freud really created in this sense is two different approaches to psychology and all the social sciences. In one, the usual, there is an intellectual examination of bodies of evidence, in the time-honored techniques of history, economics, etc. The observer remains unexamined. In the other, there is first of all a detailed study of the observer (personal analysis), and then the objective data are assessed. It is this dichotomy, which few understand, that has led to such wide divergences in the data of the social sciences. The recent attack on Margaret Mead's views on Samoa by Derek Freeman, which is really a savage attack on her, is a case in point. She was not an analyst, but remained close to the analytic point of view all her life. Incidentally this is one of the many examples in anthropology where two observers have come out with two different sets of facts, justifying Roheim's suggestion that all anthropologists should first be analyzed before going out into the field; otherwise their personal prejudices may color the material beyond recognition.

Even quantitatively, Freud's sheer productivity after his self-analysis is enormous. Of the 23 volumes in the Standard Edition (the 24th is the Index), only three cover the period to 1899, when his self-analysis was still in progress; the other twenty come after his analysis. Thus in his case it can certainly be said that for Freud the analysis removed his blocks and allowed an enormous surge of creativity.

Sergei Pankejeff, more familiarly known as the Wolf Man (his name was finally revealed when he died at the age of 92; the reasons for keeping it secret are as mysterious as many of the other aspects of this case, e.g. why he was kept on as a showpiece for psychoanalysis) was in a state of complete collapse when he first consulted Freud in 1910. A Viennese journalist by the name of Karin Obholzer recently (1982) published her conversations with the Wolf Man toward the end of his life, so that we have a pretty complete record of his analytic career.

The Wolf Man (1971) had an exhaustive analysis with Freud, and a number of analyses, or analytic experiences after he left Freud. Even in his old age he was in contact with Eissler (who is identified in the Obholzer book as Dr. E., keeper of the Freud Archives), who apparently on his annual summer visits to Vienna had some sessions with him, and gave him a lot of practical advice. Obholzer tries to see this as proof of the failure of Freud's work, but this conclusion no one who knows the nature of psychotherapy and the human condition will share.

When he first came to Freud, the Wolf Man was in a state of total disintegration. He was a millionaire Russian, travelling around Europe with a whole retinue, including his own physician, the one who introduced him to Freud. In current terms he was completely unable to function, having dropped out of graduate school some time before. He was 23 when he started with Freud. In the first session he offered to have rectal intercourse with Freud and then to defecate on his head.[15] (This is based on a letter from Ferenczi; in the Obholzer book the Wolf Man denies this, further states that he was never in correspondence with Jones, and that he never really had many symptoms anyhow; the journalist fails to distinguish between the denials of an old man who was trying to make a play for her, and even ordinary lapses of memory in a man in his late eighties.)

After a successful analysis, and the loss of his fortune in the Russian revolution, the Wolf Man settled in Vienna, where he remained the rest of his life. When he came back to Vienna after the war in 1919, he felt better but Freud induced him to stay for some extra (free!) treatment for constipation. In his talks with Obholzer the Wolf Man is bitter at Freud for this extra treatment, saying that had

he gone back to Odessa in those troubled times he could have sal-
vaged his personal fortune.

Eventually the Wolf Man became a lawyer, working for an insurance firm until his retirement in 1950. He also became an
amateur painter, though he had never shown any ability in this area
before and in the 1930's wrote a number of articles for insurance
journals.[16] Though his paintings have been praised by Muriel Gard-
ner, the analyst in closest touch with him after Freud, they have
never been displayed. However, for our present discussion it is
significant that he developed two new creative outlets which he had
not had before analysis—writing and painting.

In this connection it is interesting to note that he relates that at one
point in the analysis with Freud he was preoccupied with the idea of
becoming a painter (Freud does not mention this in his discussion,
which confines itself to the infantile neurosis). In a most un-
Freudian manner, Freud advised him against this, expressing the
opinion that although he probably had the ability he would not find
the profession satisfying.

> He believed that the contemplative nature of the artist was not
> foreign to me but that the rational (he once called me a "dia-
> lectician") predominated. He suggested that I should strive for
> a sublimation that would also absorb my intellectual interest
> completely. It was on this occasion that he told me that his
> youngest son had also intended to become a painter, but had
> then dropped the idea and switched over to architecture.[17]

Freud further opined that one should regard painting as a luxury,
pursuing it as an amateur, or else take it very seriously and achieve
something really great, since to be a mediocrity in this field would
give no satisfaction. As is well known, Freud never wanted any of
his children to become physicians, but did want them to become
lawyers (one did—Martin). Talk of countertransference! In spite of
Freud's admonition, the Wolf Man did later become a painter; as
noted, how well he did we do not know.

To recapitulate: What is important is that in this 23-year-old man,
so badly crippled by neurosis, new creative potential emerged as a
result of successful analysis.

Another quotation from Freud by the Wolf Man is interesting. He
says that Freud once told him[18] that even when the repressed
becomes conscious and when an analysis could be regarded as successful, this does not automatically bring about the patient's

recovery. Freud compared the situation with the purchase of a rail ticket. The ticket, which is produced by the analysis, makes the trip possible; but the patient has to use it to make the journey. This, too, is relevant to the discussion here. Successful analysis makes creative actions possible, but the patient still has to undertake them himself. Of the many literary people whom Freud analyzed the best known is the poetess Hilda Doolittle, or H.D. as she is known. She lived from 1886 to 1961. Her analysis with Freud (not entirely a systematic one because of the chaotic political conditions) lasted from 1933 to 1934. She has written a number of accounts of her analysis, but because of her penchant for poetic expression it is not easy to get an objective reaction to what happened with Freud.

As her life is told by Janice Robinson (1982), H.D. was born into Moravian family in Bethlehem, Pennsylvania. Her father was a professor of astronomy. After a rather typically repressed childhood, she fell in love with the famous poet Ezra Pound and wanted to marry him. Her family was opposed, her father considering Pound a "nomad". Nevertheless, she followed Pound to Europe and became "equivocally" engaged to him a few years later. She also began to write poetry, becoming one of the founders of the "imagist" school, which emphasized precise, sharp images. Although she expected to marry Pound he suddenly deserted her for more fertile ground when he met Dorothy Shakespear, who afforded him more access to important literary circles in England at that time. She accepted the outright rejection with outer equanimity, although she said it drove her to "a forceful effort toward artistic achievement."[19] But Pound (a sadistic lover who later identified with fascism and spent years in a mental hospital) remained a great influence in her life. In fact, from her biography it seems that she always remained involved with him at some level.

Her life was not a happy one, but one dominated by strong men. She married a poet Richard Aldington, from whom she separated after several years. Later she had a romantic fling with D.H. Lawrence, who seems to have been the father of her only child, Perdita (a curious name: "lost"). But Lawrence also deserted her soon, and never had the same force in her life as her first great love, Pound.

In desperation she then turned to a woman, Bryher, with whom she had some lesbian experiences. Bryher was wealthy (H.D. suffered financial problems all her life) and helped H.D. out in various ways. It was Bryher who paid for the first part of her analysis with Freud.

Not surprisingly, with such a background the transference was strong and positive. She had had some previous analysis with Hanns Sachs, so she was used to the rules. Following her first session, she wrote that she did not want to lie down with a "napkin for the head". Freud, she says, then said to her: "I see you are going to be very difficult. Now although it is against the rules, I will tell you something: *YOU WERE DISAPPOINTED, AND YOU ARE DISAPPOINTED, IN ME.*" I then let out a howl, and screamed, "but do you not realize that you are everything, you are priest, you are magician." He said: "No, it is you who are poet and magician."[20]

Her biographer writes that her outward circumstances did not change immediately as a result of her work with Freud, but in time she began to live a new life. She had been subtly transformed through Freud's affirmation of her (in contrast to Pound's shabby mishandling), even if she did not accept everything he wrote and said as gospel. Her record of her first month of analysis has been recorded in her book *Advent,* signifying her experience of it as a second birth. Freud again showed some countertransference when a few months after she started he placed a statue of Pallas Athene with a missing spear in her hands.

How successful the analysis was in terms of her inner happiness is impossible to judge from the published material. She did feel better and eventually broke the homosexual liaison with Bryher. But she never again related to another man, holding on to her attachments to Pound and then Freud. There was a relationship with an American analyst Walter Schmideberg, but its nature is not spelled out. In 1945 she had a breakdown, for which she was forcibly hospitalized and given shock treatment. Of this treatment she wrote "I was never really afraid, until that 'shock treatment', then I was so damned mad, I sort of got well."[21]

In spite of that, after an accident some years later, she was hospitalized in a Swiss clinic, where she seemed to have received physical therapy for the illness: abdominal surgery and later a broken hip complicated by a bone illness. She was in a Swiss lakeside clinic in Kuesnacht (where Jung, for whom she had no use, also lived) for most of the last eight years of her life. In addition to the medical therapy she received psychotherapy (or analysis?) from a Dr. Erich Heydt, but the nature of this therapy is not described in the biography.

Looking at her life, she had a repressed religious background dominated by a strong father in a scientific area which she could not enter. Then Pound came along, and her attachment to him remained all through her life, in spite of his complete desertion and other sadistic actions. Next came Lawrence for a few years, then a homosexually tinged liaison with Bryher. Finally the analysis with Freud, whom she then revered until she died. But her psychic equilibrium does not seem to have been very great, since she had one forced hospitalization, and spent the last eight years of her life in a clinic where she received some psychotherapy. However, she did express the feeling over and over that the analyst had changed her inner outlook on life.

As for her creativity, it seems to have benefited enormously from the analysis. Where before she had been dominated by Pound and his views, later by Lawrence, now she went her own way. She wrote extensively and in 1960 became the first woman to receive the Award of Merit Medal for Poetry of the American Academy of Arts and Letters. The quality of her poetry is difficult to judge, especially in such a subjective field. Martindale (1975) has shown how evanescent eminence is in this field. In his study it is seen that a certain degree of regression (or incomprehensibility) is highly valued, but if it goes too far it is rejected. (This observation certainly applies to her lifelong hero Pound). In any case, less important than our judgment is her own feeling of satisfaction with her work, and this was indeed considerable. In that sense the analysis did release great energies which had been kept in check before by childish submission to sadistic father-figures.

Freud was evidently fond of writers, and three others could be mentioned in this context. Marie Bonaparte (the "Princess"— 1882-1962), Lou-Andreas Salome, (1861-1936) and James Strachey (1887-1967). All of them were writers before they entered analysis, though of no particular stature. Then came the analysis with Freud or the contact with him (Strachey's is described as a cross between an analysis and a series of chats), while Lou-Andreas' is described as a "pupil". Nor was the analysis of Marie Bonaparte conducted with the usual analytic rigor; Freud was obviously thrilled with having the idea of a princess as a real friend. All three then became competent analysts late in life (all in their 40's) and wrote extensively on analytic topics. Marie Bonaparte also wrote a book about her dog Topsy, but its only claim to fame is that Freud devoted some time to its translation. For the rest, all gave up their endeavors to write fiction in favor of practicing analysis.

In this transformation from writer to analyst, it is to be noted that none of the three had or have any particular standing as writers.

Hence their shift to psychoanalysis as their main occupation and preoccupation could have come out of this awareness as well as out of their fascination for analytic work. In any case, for the thesis of this paper the point is that all became more creative as a result of the analysis, even if the creativity did lead them in a different direction from the one originally intended.

We may also mention a number of prominent analysts or psychiatrists who were analyzed by Freud—Heinz Hartmann, Roy Grinker, Abram Kardiner, Joseph Wortis, Smiley Blanton, among others. All of these men led productive lives as analysts or therapists, though all in different directions. This too is noteworthy, since it illustrates Freud's remark to the Wolf Man: "The analyst provides the ticket for the ride, but the patient has to take the ride."

OTHER CREATIVE INDIVIDUALS

There is a considerable amount of literature available relating in one way or another to the analysis or therapy of artists or other prominent persons in modern times, but the results are highly individual. Marilyn Monroe, who had two of the best analysts in the country to help her, committed suicide when her analyst (Greenson) could not come to the phone. Tennessee Williams had five years of analysis with little effect. Clifford Odets changed little in analysis. On the other hand, many well-known and lesser-known figures have had most successful analyses, but do not feel driven to write up their experiences. Moss Hart is supposed to have written *Lady in the Dark* as a gift to his analyst who had helped him enormously, but the play does not tell us anything about him.

Judging from my own experience, I would say that in general analysis removes the blocks which have hampered the creative individual before treatment. What happens then varies widely with the individual. Some are satisfied with the new freedom: others seek another field; still others at times try to become analysts themselves. The question of why the analytic process should in general be helpful in the release of creativity will be considered in more detail.

THOSE WHO GIVE UP THEIR CREATIVE OUTLET

We have already mentioned the great fear of the creative artist that analysis will somehow rob him of his creativity. This virtually never happens, in my experience. What does happen is that a creative outlet may turn out to cover up a neurotic problem. Once the problem is resolved, then the creative outlet no longer has the same drive or meaning for the individual. Even this rarely happens, as far as I can see. But it does occur at times. Creativity after all is as broad as life itself. Every creative individual knows that no matter how competent he is, the act of creation involves some unusual effort, not infrequently some pain or suffering. In the Fried study it was noted that many artists threw away a lot of théir work. Evidently they were dissatisfied with it, but throwing it away could not have made them happy.

On the other hand, returning to the question of what happens to the creative man outside analysis, we know that many give up their creative outlets out of a sense of frustration or because they are not well received, or for other reasons. It is rare to see any creative individual who does not experience blocks of some kind during his or her productivity.

Furthermore, the creative artist, especially in our times, often sets himself impossible tasks. Recall the narcissistic grandiosity which Fried found in her artists. Every novel must be a masterpiece, every painting must be bought by the Metropolitan, every composition must be performed by the Philharmonic, etc. In such an atmosphere it is inevitable that there will be setbacks and disappointments. The example of Fitzgerald was cited earlier: after a while he gave up creative writing altogether and went to work for Hollywood, not because of the money alone, but because he had lost the creative spark through his drinking and self-destructive way of living.

Furthermore, as Rank pointed out a long time ago, many artists are less interested in the art itself than in the Bohemian life which it permits them to live. An example could be cited here of many modern artists whose primary interest seems to be in shocking the public rather than in producing anything. E.g. Lucas Samaras, a contemporary artist, who once wanted to be a psychiatrist, invites people to take off their clothes and sit nude in his studio. He also likes to inject himself into his pictures, though the gain in artistic excellence is hard to see.[22] With many of his later productions, such as the bicycle wheel, Marcel Duchamp seemed to be pulling the leg of the spectators. The Dada movement in Germany after WWI is another good example: to cut out unrelated pieces of paper, and put them together, does in some way express the horror and senselessness of the world in 1920, but what could its artistic value be? Had such cases come to analysis they might very well have been abandoned by their proponents. We touch here upon the vast problems connected with what art really is, which cannot be discussed further in this paper.

To return to the analytic scene. Here is one good example of how an artistic outlet can cover up a neurotic problem. Sally, a promiscuous woman who was an artist (this case is described in more detail in my book *The Intimate Hour*) had developed a hobby of buying old tables, remaking them as if they were new and selling them at a profit. At the same time she was extremely promiscuous, terribly unhappy with her four-year-old son, and caught in a bad marriage. In the course of the analysis she realized that her actions with the old tables was a substitute for the wish to reshape herself; she was the old table, reshaped and presented as new. With this realization she eventually gave up the activity. In the end she resolved her problems by having another child and establishing a happier family life. The artistic urge however remained strong. Later in life, when the children were older, she went back to another artistic pursuit.

THOSE WHO DEVELOP AN ARTISTIC ABILITY

Since analysis is so intimately involved with creativity, it is a natural expectation of many that it will produce some creative urge in them. This does happen, but it is rather unusual. It is useful to inquire into the theoretical reasons why this should be so.

First an example from the literature and then from my practice. Hannah Green, author of *I Never Promised You a Rose Garden,* was a chronic schizophrenic who would have been abandoned by any ordinary psychiatrist. But it was her good fortune to meet up with Frieda Fromm-Reichmann. The extraordinary capacity for devotion which Fromm-Reichmann had for her patients helped Hannah Green to overcome her schizophrenic psychosis and after many years of treatment come back to a fairly normal life. She was even able in her book to describe much of the therapeutic process. Eventually she became a writer on psychiatric topics; at one time she was awarded the Fromm-Reichmann prize, which must have been a special pleasure for her.

One of my patients, a young woman of 22, came into analysis in a highly regressed state. The immediate precipitating factor was that she went to work wearing two slips, one on top of the other, instead of a slip and a dress. At the same time she had her share of narcissistic grandiosity, insisting that she was as great a writer as Shakespeare. When this was questioned, since she had never written anything, she replied: "Before Shakespeare wrote his plays, nobody knew what he could do either".

The patient was in analysis for many years, and improved gradually, almost imperceptibly. At one time in fact I had the impression (later proved to be groundless) that she was brain damaged. One of the factors that helped her to improve was that she was brought up in such a state of severe dependency that the dependency on the analyst was felt as a great boon.

In the course of her treatment, she developed an interest in sculpture. Here she discovered some unexpected talent. She pursued the field, and eventually achieved a considerable amount of progress in it. She also improved intellectually, and acquired a doctorate in fine arts. Her persistence paid off.

In both these cases the talent that came to the fore had not been suspected. Outside analysis this happens too of course; e.g. there is the phenomenon of Grandma Moses—who in her 70's became an outstanding artist. Colleagues who work with the aged have told me that there is a Grandma Moses in every installation for the aged. This may or may not be true, but certainly there are many people who later in life, or after retirement, develop unusual abilities—perhaps because they have finally been relieved of the everyday grind. This does not happen too often, but that it happens is in itself of note. In a somewhat similar vein, Bleuler (1978) reports that sometimes backward schizophrenics after 40 years in the hospital, snap out of their psychosis and are almost normal in the last five or ten years of their lives. This reinforces one of the major theses of psychoanalysis, that we are still in the dark about human potentialities.

The creativogenic environment plays a role here too. One of my patients (Beverly, or "Evil Incarnate" in my book *The Intimate Hour*) had been through three hospitalizations for schizophrenia. As she came out of the psychosis she started to write her memoirs, producing a book of some 200 pages which was a starkly realistic portrayal of what it is like to be in a mental hospital. No publisher would touch it, because it lacked the glitter and magic which could make such books popular. After several tries she eventually gave up her literary endeavors.

THOSE INDIFFERENT TO CREATIVITY

Finally there are many analysands who express indifference to any aspect of the creative process. They wish to get over their problems, move on to a happier kind of life. In these people there is an inner creativity which has great momentum, but they lack the impetus for outer creativity. Many times they do not have great talent in any sphere. In other instances they are sufficiently happy in their love lives that they do not seek anything else. After all, if love and work are the goals, or the core of the analytic ideal, some find a solution in work, some in love, some in a combination of the two. Furthermore, the realities hit them in the face too. Prominent publishers, it is said, receive as many as 5000 unsolicited manuscripts a year; they do not have the editorial staff which would allow them to read more than a small fraction of these. So again talent may go undiscovered, and the person adjusts himself to the reality.

DISCUSSION

Our primary concern is with those who have talent, are creative and come to analysis for resolution of their personal problems. What happens to their creativity? The general answer has already been suggested: blocks are overcome, and they make better use of the talent that has always been theirs. Some people who have used an artistic outlet neurotically may give it up. But by and large those who are creative do not lose any of their gifts in the course of analysis. On some occasions new talents are uncovered, and finally there are many in analysis who are not interested in creativity and do not learn to pursue any outlet.

The major conclusion then is that analysis removes blocks, but does not, except for some unusual individuals, produce talent which did not exist before analysis. The problem now is to explain these findings dynamically.

In essence, creativity and analysis begin with the same procedure; say or do whatever comes to mind. In analysis we call it free association; in art it is called inspiration. The analyst then helps the analysand to order his associations so that he gains insight into his unconscious; the artist moulds his inspirations into some product which is intelligible to others. Hilda Doolittle tells us that in her analysis with Freud she associated with images, in much the same way as she had written poetry. And just as she learned to regulate her images in her poetry she learned to make sense of her image-associations in her analysis.

As we know, one of the most common reactions to the question What comes to mind? is: nothing. The analysand resists; he cannot share his associations with the analyst. Likewise the artist looking for inspiration has many thoughts or ideas, but does not quite know how to put them into proper form. Words, words, words, Sartre once said, revealing his own frustration with his literary output.

Once an artist was referred to me for a Rorschach examination. As soon as he saw the cards, he said'' ''Oh, I know that, I used to do that when I was a kid.'' Then he opened his pen, dripped the ink on the paper, and created images of his own. His inspiration was of course highly original, but did not help in evaluating his personality because there was no basis for comparison, as there is in the ordinary Rorschach cards.

As a rule the artist does not know where his inspiration comes from and often it takes him time to decide what to do with it. Usually the artist opposes the analytic idea that inspiration can be explained just like any other psychological phenomenon. He prefers to see his inspiration as a ''gift from the Gods''. This is a major reason why so many artists oppose analysis. The Russian writer Nabokov, e.g. was strongly anti-analytic, claiming that he had his way of doing things, while Freud had his; obviously he was in competition with Freud.

The gift from the Gods is another description of narcissism; often healthy narcissism. But still narcissism. In another paper I have tried to show that the artist in his childhood experiences approval for his narcissistic activities; this approval then leads to more narcissistic pleasure, then to more approval. This whole sequence leads him to learn the artistic craft, whatever the medium may be (Fine, 1980).

While artists work, and often work incessantly (cf. the quotation from Chaim Gross earlier in this paper) they usually prefer to emphasize their inspiration more than their work. Yet no matter how inspired the idea may be, it still has to be worked out. Schneider uses the phrases; creative thrust (id—inspiration) and creative mastery (ego—working out). Similarly in analysis: there is the creative thrust—the free association, the dream, then the creative mastery, working out what this is all about. Many analysands make the mistake of thinking that all they have to do is produce associations, even resenting the analyst's attempt to make sense out of what they are saying.

This inspiration in the artist then represents narcissistic pleasure. Since no one likes to give up any narcissistic gratification, the artist sees the analyst as his enemy who will take away the pleasure; the superego in short. And of course many times the parents did behave in such a way, since parents often frown upon their children's artistic endeavors: to become an artist under such circumstances requires a heroic effort; it can be done but it is rare.

Since the analyst may remove the narcissistic pleasure, the threat that the analyst poses becomes clear. As a result the artist stays away.

Another dynamic factor that plays a role is the transference constellation. In *Tender Is the Night,* Fitzgerald unconsciously described his transference wish: to drag the analyst down to his own level and destroy him. In many cases this is even quite close to consciousness. The consequence is that the analysis is given up and a hostile attitude takes its place.

In one instance a comedian entered analysis without any money. After a few weeks he confessed his monetary plight, and left. Then he went into his major resistance: he began to imitate the analyst in social gatherings. Since he was a good mimic, he was entertaining. But it did not help him with his problems; today some forty years later, he is still making fun of the analyst, and still suffering with his neurotic problems.

These considerations also explain the positive attitude that so many artists display to analysis. For while the danger of losing their narcissistic pleasure is acute, after the early stages many realize that it is a chimera. They then enter into the process with great gusto and abandon. And since they are more used to probing into their unconscious (inspiration) they produce more material, pay more attention to it, and get more out of the analysis. The blocks that appeared in the artistic production are the same as the blocks that reappear in the analysis. Once they are understood in the analysis, they can also be tackled in real life.

An actor who had had nine months of analysis with a woman to whom he could not talk consulted me. He began by saying: "I don't think that you can help me because I can't talk." I replied: "You're talking now." This was enough to lift whatever inhibitions he was suffering from at that time, and he began to talk quite freely. A similar problem had arisen in his professional life; he had lost his voice during a stage performance, and had to leave the show.

Why does new talent not arise more often as a result of analysis? It does, but creativity is much more than mere talent. Every creative person has a background of many years of hard work at his field, whatever that may be. And this background is every bit as important as the talent. However, here too the artist tends to deceive himself, relying more on his self-image as an inspired person than on a self-image as a hard-working person. In fact, we even have different expressions for work blocks in normal and in creative individuals. If the normal individual does not want to work or cannot work, we say he needs a vacation; if the artist does not want to work, we say that he is blocked.

RECAPITULATION

Without going through the whole argument again I would merely like to stress here that the major effect of psychoanalysis on the creative individual, apart from straightening out his love life, as with all analysands, is to remove the blocks to his artistic productivity. When these blocks occur, however, they are seen as blocks only in persons who have a large backlog of ability in the field which he or she is pursuing. Because of the lack of such a backlog, new talent is not often uncovered within the analytic process. However, at times it is. Because of that we should always maintain our confidence in the analytic process. The analyst provides the ticket: the patient has to use it. Even if he does not use it the first or second time he may do so eventually. Our faith in human potential, so badly crippled by our hate culture, should never be abandoned.

NOTES

1. Fried, p. vii.
2. Fried, p. viii.
3. Fried, p. ix.
4. Le Vot, p. 357.
5. Mizener, p. 377.
6. Le Vot, p. 294.
7. Le Vot, p. 294.
8. Le Vot, p. 301.
9. Mortensen, p. 737.
10. Simpson, p. 87.
11. Simpson, p. 50.
12. Simpson, p. 159.
13. Berryman, Henry's Fate, p. 87.
14. Brenman-Gibson, p. 160.
15. Jones, Vol. 2, p. 274.
16. Wolf Man, p. 114.
17. Wolf Man, pp. 144-145.
18. Wolf Man, p. 148.
19. Robinson, p. 26.
20. Robinson, p. 278.
21. Robinson, p. 341.
22. Gruen, 1976.

BIBLIOGRAPHY

Ammons, C. H. and Ammons, R.B. 1962. How to Prevent Genius: McCurdy Revisited. *Proceedings of the Montana Academy of Sciences,* 2, 145-152.

Anzieu, D. 1975. *L'Auto-Analyse de Freud.* Paris: Presses Universitaires de France.

Arieti, S. 1976. *Creativity: The Magic Synthesis.* New York: Basic Books.

Berryman, J. 1977. *Henry's Fate.* New York: Farrar, Straus and Giroux.

Bertin, C. 1982. *Marie Bonaparte: A Life.* New York: Harcourt, Brace and Jovanovic.

Bleuler, M. 1978. *The Schizophrenic Disorders.* New Haven: Yale.

Brenman-Gibson, M. 1981. *Clifford Odets: American Playwright.* New York: Atheneum.

Bychowski, G. 1951. Metapsychology of Artistic Creation. *Psychoanalytic Quarterly,* 20, 592-602.

Fine, R. 1979. *A History of Psychoanalysis.* New York: Columbia U. Press.

Fine, R. 1979. *The Intimate Hour.* New York: Avery Publishing Co.

Fine, R. 1980. Work, Depression and Creativity. *Psychological Reports.* 46, 1195-1121.

Freud, S. 1905. Psychopathic Characters on the Stage. *Standard Edition,* VII, 305-310.

Freud, S. 1908. Creative Writers and Daydreaming. *Standard Edition.* IX, 141-154.

Freud, S. 1910. Leonardo da Vinci. *Standard Edition,* XI, 59-137.

Fried, E. et al. 1964. *Artistic Productivity and Mental Health.* Springfield, Ill.: C.C. Thomas.

Gedo, M. 1982. *Art as Autobiography.* Chicago: U. of Chicago Press.

Green, H. 1964. *I Never Promised You a Rose Garden.* New York: Holt, Rinehart and Winston.

Gruen, J. 1976. The Apocalyptic Disguises of Lucas Samaras. *Art News,* April, 35-37.

Guilford, J.P. 1967. *The Nature of Human Intelligence.* New York: McGraw-Hill.

Jones, E. 1953-1957. *The Life and Work of Sigmund Freud.* New York: Basic Books.

Le Vot, A. 1983. *F. Scott Fitzgerald.* New York: Doubleday.

Martindale, C. 1975. *Romantic Progression.* New York: Wiley.

Matson, K. 1980. *Short Lives.* New York: William Morrow.

Mizener, A. 1978. F. Scott Fitzgerald. In *Encyclopedia Britannica.* 7, 377-378.

Mortensen, B.M. 1978. August Strindberg. In *Encyclopedia Britannica.* 17, 737-738.

Niederland, W. 1976. Psychoanalytic Approaches to Creativity. *Psychoanalytic Quarterly.* 45, 185-212.

Obholzer, K. 1982. *The Wolf Man: Sixty Years Later.* New York: Continuum.

Rank, O. 1932. *Art and the Artist.* New York: Tudor.

Robinson, J.S. 1982. *H.D. The Life and Work of an American Poet.* Boston: Houghton Mifflin.

Rothenberg, A. and Hausman, C.R. eds. 1976. *The Creativity Question.* Durham, N.C.: Duke U. Press.

Sharpe, E. 1935. Similar and Divergent Unconscious Determinants Underlying the Sublimitations of Pure Art and Pure Science. *Int. Journal of Psychoanalysis.* 16, 186-202.

Wolf Man. 1971. *The Wolf Man.* New York: Basic Books.

Psychoanalysis in Groups:
The Primacy of the Individual

Irwin L. Kutash
Alexander Wolf

INTRODUCTION

Alexander Wolf, in 1938, began psychoanalytic treatment in a group setting. In 1947 five groups of patients were in treatment and now over thirty-five years later some of these same groups, being open ended, are still being eagerly sought out and utilized. Psychoanalysis in groups, however, has been relegated by some of today's group psychodynamic therapists to an historical role. This is unfortunate because this type of treatment, as shall be illustrated, is more relevant today than ever for some very important individual and societal reasons. Most importantly, because psychoanalysis in groups stresses individual differences and individuality as opposed to group dynamics or group process. Individuality can lead to greater group cohesiveness than efforts toward homogeneity since a person needs to appreciate himself before he can truly appreciate others.

The thrust of psychoanalysis in groups is that the creative growth of the individual ego is primary. Group psychotherapy is a misnomer for a technique that, while conducted in a group, is designed to aid an individual. It is treatment of ailing individuals in a group setting, not treatment of ailing groups. Only individuals have egos, internalized object relations, introjected parents or, for that matter, intrapsychic dynamics.

This paper contains the basic principle of psychoanalysis in groups that the individual ego is primary. It is also intended to challenge the emerging group dynamic approaches and to deal with what we consider the key issue in psychoanalytic group therapy today. The issues central to our approach that will be covered include the primacy of the individual versus mass man, individual within the group versus group-as-a-whole approaches, homogeneous or heterogeneous groups and closed versus open ended groups.

PRIMACY OF THE INDIVIDUAL VERSUS MASS MAN

There are forces at work within our society which contribute toward preventing the development of autonomous egos, contribute to their inhibition and foster a pseudo-homogeneity. Examples include crowding out of individual initiative with its limitations of choices, over-mediazation, automation with its assembly line mentality and breaking down of family structure. For more ample coverage of the link between modern day stresses and personality see Kutash and Schlesinger (1980). It is clear that excessive individuation is more and more considered an illness in a crowded group oriented society. These same tendencies need to be resisted in therapy groups. The authors have observed crowded, automated groups, groups where group themes limited individual choices, the ignoring of mother and father transferences in groups as if familial influence can now be neglected. In other words a person drowning in the homogeneity of modern day society may find himself in an overcrowded group, being videotaped and tape recorded, expected to shift quickly to "group values" and to follow an externally imposed pace of group instead of evolving and unfolding as individual ego growth is fostered.

If the contention that present day society is "drowning the individual in homogeneity" is accepted it is not surprising then that a generation of group therapists raised in such a society should fashion group therapy approaches that can do the same thing. Therapy fashioned to cure a person from the ills of a sick family or sick society ought not to rely on joint group mood, consensus or interaction to influence and cure a sick member. The exploration and working through of the intrapsychic unconscious pathology of each individual member remains the more difficult but most valid goal of treatment. The group simply provides a more economical setting and one where the possibility of relationships with peer figures as well as authority figures is present to be dealt with, where both intrapsychic and interpersonal processes occur and where "brother-sister" as well as "mother-father" transferences develop and can be analyzed.

Group dynamic approaches utilizing such techniques as consensual validation can exert strong influences on group members toward conformity or uniformity of thinking, feeling, and behavior. The acceptance of group uniformity can only manifestly satisfy the needs of those who have always felt different and isolated but frustrates the more basic need for independent ego. This conflict between individuation and the need for a sense of inclusion is engendered by group approaches with group goals as opposed to group approaches with the aim of fostering individuality and a sense of differentiated identity. In the latter approach, each person discovers his own goals, which prove mutually beneficial in complementary difference. The primary purpose of psychoanalysis in groups is psychoanalysis of the individual within a group. The group leader must help to protect the member with weaker egos from the danger of incorporation by the group-as-a-whole for successful psychoanalysis within the group.

The Talmud advises "that if someone says you are drunk, you can shrug your shoulders. If two persons say you are drunk, stop and listen. But if three say you are drunk, lie down." These and similar stories have been used to illustrate the powerful positive influence of the consensual validation process that can occur in a group setting. The authors would see this as an illustration as well of a danger in the group process. What if these people say the individual is drunk and he is not? The weak ego is further buried. A more valuable experience may occur when an individual correctly tells a group "you are all mistaken", when the individual is in touch with his internal experience and has the strength to withstand the consensus and even the leader's opinion. The group, rather than suppressing the ego, at times with a short term behavioral gain, has provided the laboratory for the individual to gain ego strength. This has been observed by one of us (see Wolf, 1981) to be a quality of genius: freedom from the tyranny of the homogenized consensus. In some cases, a group can be a composite of eight weak egos supporting each other to survive but unfortunately not to grow. This has been termed "malequilibrium" in group by one of us (Kutash 1980) and will be discussed further later.

An example of a group atmosphere where individuality is cherished over consensus is illustrated in the following case:

A group member was offered a new job in another state and asked the group what to do? Each member in his own way told him to trust himself, not to listen to parents, bosses or even the group but to discover what he wanted to do, separate from complying or rebelling against others. This patient then analyzed the situation independent of his struggle with introjected parents and moved forward on his road to recovery. This encouraged the others to trust their own ego. The group atmosphere was such that the members did not feel compelled to arrive at a consensus that might have overwhelmed the individual ego involved.

E. James Anthony (1971) wrote that just as "the superego is soluble in alcohol, it's also soluble—as Le Bon, McDougall and Freud pointed out—in the ecstasies occasioned by close group interaction, but there is always a hangover when reality once again asserts itself." To this the authors would add the further warning: the ego may be equally vulnerable. The weaker the ego, the more suppressed it is in homogeneous group responses. While acknowledging that, at best, there are some positives in homogeneous group responses and it is valuable when patients relate to each other positively and support one another's weak egos, such mental sustenance should not be confused with psychoanalytic treatment. Furthermore, in some group dynamic approaches lies the potential for ego damage when the leader does not analyze peer pressure. Psychoanalysis in groups makes the claim that the whole is less than the sum of the parts but that is only because the parts are so very precious. The gems must not be lost in the tiara.

INDIVIDUAL-WITHIN-THE-GROUP VERSUS GROUP-AS-A-WHOLE APPROACHES TO GROUP TREATMENT

To begin with, the basic difference between psychoanalysis in groups and group dynamic approaches has been termed a difference between dyadic psychoanalytic techniques and group specific factors techniques. This is not the case. Psychoanalysis in groups is an interactive technique involving eight to ten individuals with a leader as a facilitator. Group dynamic approaches are often dyadic, or an interaction between a leader and a projectively homogenized group ego. Where the difference truly lies is that the individual-within-the-group approach focuses on understanding intrapsychic dynamic patterns, with group interaction used to facilitate insights leading to more wholesome ego development and interpersonal relations. Group-as-a-whole approaches focus on interactive patterns within the matrix of the group, believing in their generalizability to more fulfilling outside livings. The authors believe that the first approach leads to both more pain and more pleasure in one's life outside the group as a person comes to know and appreciate himself and others as individuals, while the latter facilitates more comfort while decreasing the possibility of these emotional peaks and valleys. The choice becomes philosophical as well as judgmental. Does therapy aim to help the person be himself or fit in as its priority? If these are the choices in emphasis, the patient should be aware of it before treatment begins.

Furthermore, a sharp distinction needs to be made between the therapist's recognition of group trends, the enrichment of his knowledge of the group as a group, and his activity as a therapist for patients who constitute the group. There are various kinds of groups, therapy groups as well as other sorts of groups. One may then use the group in order to study group dynamics or to accomplish other purposes such as education. Or one may use the group therapeutically. If we focus our attention on group dynamic processes, we cannot also at the same time easily attend diagnosis, psychopathology, individual psychodynamics, dream analysis, resistance, transference and countertransference reactions, provocative roles, multiple reactivities, and other relevant parameters. Concentration on group dynamics can become a way of anthropomorphizing the group while rationalizing that treatment equates with the elaboration of group dynamic processes.

The therapist is involved in a process of levelling, when he expects a group to function as if it were a uniform group. Such obscuring of disparity applied to the family group would repudiate the reality of the difference between parent and child, between older child and younger child, between girls and boys, between father and mother. Although the family may seem to function as a unit, it is unreal to view it as if it were constituted of mirror images within the family structure. These unlikenesses are rejected in the implication that there is a basic family dynamic, a family unity, which contains within it no place for independent motivation, personal history, variance in one's own reaction even to the same family traditions, structure, and heritage. The second child is not entering the same family as the first child or the third child. With each birth, the family becomes a new one; where a new fragment of history is added and a new generalized structure is developed. Each succeeding child must deal with the family as a changing family. Its structure changes as distinguishable children are added to it.

On the basis of perusal of literature and our own combined experience spanning the decades from the late 30's to the 80's, the authors conclude there is still no clinical evidence demonstrating that attention to group dynamics is useful to the understanding and treatment of the patient in a group setting. A positive group climate, or what the authors term group equilibrium, can be therapeutic but what promotes individual ego development is the psychoanalytic treatment occurring within that climate. A group climate is the result of the interaction of unique individuals with their individual dynamics, but attending to group dynamics is either doing a disservice to the individual egos involved or a projected group-as-a-whole transference of the therapist. The individual is the baby, group dynamics at best the bath water, cleansing for some, drowning to others but healing to none. Healing takes more than cleansing the wound or defining the injury. Reconstructive analysis requires the treatment of the individual's psychopathology not either one collective compromise dynamic or one therapist's projection.

An illustration of the psychoanalysis in groups approach as contrasted with group-as-a-whole approaches can be found in an excerpt from a paper written for a group therapy course by a supervisee of one of us (ILK), Nattland (1983).

"On the night of the interaction to be analysed, three members are absent and two members arrive late. This sequence of interactions was selected because it involves only 3 members and one leader . . . . from the point of view of 'psychoanalysis in groups' even simple interactions involving few members rapidly tend to become complex.

A begins to discuss the tactical aspects of leaving his wife. B asks for details. A says he feels guilty and worried that he may become seriously depressed after moving out of the house. He reveals for the first time in group that he has been impotent on several occasions. B tells A she is glad he is moving out on his wife because he "has been in turmoil for so long". She continues by giving him a great deal of support. Then she expresses her feeling that A has not yet dealt with the anger and jealousy he feels for a woman with whom he had been having an affair. A ignores this comment. The leader points out that A has ignored B's last statement. A snaps at the leader and B admits that she, too, "skirts around issues." The leader persists in trying to get A to examine why he doesn't listen to others. A becomes increasingly angry and tries to close the topic by sarcastically retorting, "I'm glad I know I don't listen." A short silence occurs. C, the third present member, has been silent throughout this interaction.

"A therapist with a 'mass group process' (Bion) orientation might describe this interaction as characteristic of a basic assumption 'flight/fight' group.

"The therapist with an 'interpersonal process' orientation (Yalom) might view this same interaction as an example of a . . . maneuvering to 'solidify his unique position in the group sociogram.'

"A therapist with a psychoanalytic orientation (Wolf, Kutash) would focus on each individual and allow other members to do the same in order to uncover unconscious elements of each individual's behavior as it becomes manifest in interpersonal interaction . . . . and most importantly . . . . what is behind the action on the intrapsychic level."

Illustration of Psychoanalysis in Groups with its multiple reactivity, multiple transferences and neurotic distortions, and its attention to unconscious elements of each individual's behavior is found in this case excerpt from Kutash and Wolf (1982).

A group member was transferentially viewed by one younger male member of the group as an immovable controlling figure (his father). A second younger male group member also viewed him as very controlling and irritating but also experienced a positive feeling that he would like to help him to feel free to be less controlling (feelings he felt for his father). A younger female group member saw the person as manipulative and subtly controlling (this was like both her parents). A fourth group member saw him as talking down to her and treating her as if she were unintelligent (again like her parents); and yet a fifth group member saw him as a warm good father (the father she never had). When the first four members began to express their feelings to the fifth member, who was the recipient of so much transference, they told him how he should behave; as a group, they thus became transferentially his mother, who always did control him and tell him how to act. He vehemently resisted their efforts. Only after each father transference was explored one by one and the group came to see the defensive nature of this man's controlling behavior—warding off his own mother, while his transference to the group was clarified—did progress for many group members occur. Many individuals came to see how they related to present-day figures as people from their past.

HOMOGENEOUS OR HETEROGENEOUS GROUPS

Since treatment, in large part, constitutes analysis of transference, it is advantageous to place the patient in a group setting in which he can project father, mother and siblings as well. This can best be accomplished in the heterogeneous group. Furthermore, heterogeneous groups reflect a microcosm of society, and they tend to reproduce the family. Since the family probably ushered in the patient's neurosis, it is the logical agency for checking it. Despite the fact that, at first, many patients do not cope successfully with dissimilar character structures, the battle can best be won where it was apparently lost. In psychoanalysis in groups, the early precipitation and recognition of multiple transferences are facilitated by the presence of numbers of provocative familial figures in the persons of the various members. The presence of both sexes, therefore, incite and sharpens projection.

Once having assembled a heterogeneous group, however, the battle is not yet won. Homogeneous structure or heterogeneous structure can be a consequence of the position taken by the therapist. He may believe that mental health comes from individual concession to the group. Under these circumstances it is not the group that strives for such homogeneity, it is the therapist. For the group, given its head, even if it is originally relatively homogeneous, achieves a more wholesome heterogeneity. It's the therapist's drive for homogeneity that is the significant force. The imposition of a make-believe unity is a projection of the therapist. When the therapist turns the group as a whole into an earlier familial figure of his own, the authors term it the leader's-group-as-a-whole transference.

The treatment of diverse patients as if they were identical helps the therapist to evade the necessity for the differentiated therapy of each one. It is quite possible that he is looking for an abbreviated form of group therapy. He may expect that the group, its climate, or its dynamics will somehow heal the patient with less need on the therapist's part to intervene. He may, like the patient, hope to evade conflicts or the struggle to resolve distortions of patients at cross purposes. By ignoring their disparity or leveling them in similarity, he can be relieved of the differentiated necessity to work through their divergent problems. Some therapists fear subjecting the patient to alien experience, as if they would protect him from the new and unknown.

He may misjudge singularity as compulsive nonconformity, and uniqueness as pathological deviation. He may try to render his group homogeneously irrational with a view to establishing "therapeutic" psychoses. Here the aim is to obscure the difference between patient and therapist.

An unconscious objective in homogenizing a group may be the therapist's need to manipulate it. A group can be more readily dealt with if it is made coalescent, if it is one mind, as if this were possible, or if the individual members have been conditioned to follow. The homogeneous group may be used by the therapist to bludgeon the patient to conform to the consensual view. The group can be more adroitly handled in the mass than in the man. But if the patient is to be lost in the group, his irrationality must be stimulated, encouraged and intensified. For he will resist his immersion in homogeneity with whatever sound reserves are still available to him.

One homogeneous aim is infallibility. In this view, the therapist can be positive if the group's even tenor is unquestioned. Homogeneity then has the quality of massive conformism. It creates new problems by encouraging infectious parapraxes. The nature of psychoanalytic practice requires that we question the motivations of patients and our own as well. Otherwise we are homogeneous with their resistance. When the right to question our patients, for them to question and disagree with one another and the therapist, to be different from one another and the therapist, is disavowed, we are forced to accept homogeneity and an illusory assurance.

A pitfall the group therapist needs to guard against is the formation, in the therapeutic group, of a clique of elite patients who underline the analyst's values or manage to establish a homogeneous bias to which they demand the remaining members conform. There is a danger here of the group's becoming noxiously homogeneous, for example in its insistence that the only acceptable material for expression must be affect loaded; or in the rule that no experience of a patient outside the group is relevant; or in the dictum that historical data is immaterial and that only the here and now counts; or in the attitude that dreams are of little consequence—and a bore besides; or in the position that this or that new member is not bright enough, not up to the group level. With such a development, the therapist must analyze, as thoroughly as possible, the psychodynamics of each patient party to this autocratically harmonizing influence until the multiple individual and divergent aspirations in the group recover. Otherwise he caters exclusively to the majority and neglects the needs of the individual patient.

What often passes for concurrence in the group is itself the expression not so much of constructive cohesion as it is of diegophrenic pathology. The split ego is so characteristic of our time that many patients passively follow the more assertive leaders, lending the group the appearance of homogeneity. This manifest accordance, so liable to be sponsored by the therapist as a salutary "group climate," needs to be analyzed as it shows itself in each dominant-submissive dyad. Each group may have one or two members whose personalities strongly sway the others. They are frequently the most verbal and active, but not necessarily reparative in their insensitivity to others. In order to support weakened egos, it is a function of the therapist not to be misled by an apparent appearance of uniformity and to analyze any compulsive passivity and leadership.

The leader discriminates between patients in order to discover their different illnesses and to be able, for each, to work through the specific way to enlist their cooperation and help them resolve their disorder. By this discriminating means, the therapist gives each member particular insight, so that patients do not expect the analyst to approach them in a homogeneous way. Sometimes a therapist is disconcerted by patients' objections that he does not treat one member like the other. When the leader is sure that patients are heterogeneous and need to be treated differently, he ceases to feel disturbed by such complaints. And he soon discovers that patients stop insisting on identical treatment from him and instead appreciate his distinguishing their respective needs.

What is the role of the therapist in the face of a developing homogeneity, a common dynamic, a shared motif in his group? It is the analyst's function to accept and understand the manifest, but also to penetrate the resistive, generalized facade to each patient's concealed, unconscious, and differentiated interest.

It is important for the therapist to value multiformity, to appreciate diverse thoughts and feelings and to demonstrate to his patients the productive import to each of the heterogeneous organization. For, as group members discover the worth of parity in difference, they permit and encourage appropriate dissimilarity in others. Then the patients themselves cultivate a climate of mutual examination that is cordial to unlikeness. This receptivity toward divergence encourages each to unfold his particularity, which in turn enriches the group experience of all. The group's interest in the discordant view fosters a medium of friendly candor in which the patient can expose himself and have more choice in determining his destiny. A patient is helped more by learning to cherish his differences or individuality than to be comforted by his sameness or conformity.

An excerpt from a case illustrative of a danger in a homogeneous group and of Group Malequilibrium when group members are all comfortable with each other but do not in any way challenge each other's defenses can be found in Kutash and Wolf (1982).

> A woman patient was placed in a group and arrived at her first meeting with a long cigarette holder and a very theatrical air and dress. After attending the session, she told the therapist, "This is not my kind of people, haven't you a group of people who have more in common with me?" The therapist, who was seeing a number of artists and theatre people, was about to start a new group. He invited this woman and several other patients who seemed compatible into the group. Everyone immediately hit it off, laughed, joked, and had a marvelous time. No one talked about themselves, their feelings, associations, or their dreams.

The group was eventually disbanded and its members placed in more heterogeneous groups.

CLOSED VERSUS OPEN ENDED GROUPS

Many schemas have emerged to describe phases of group development since the group process surge began. Some of these include: Bennis and Shepard (1956) who included a dependence and an interdependence phase taking the group from an initial preoccupation with power relationships and leader authority to a concern with intimacy among peers; Martin and Hill (1957) who in six phases saw the group as evolving from "autistic" to a more mature phase of interpersonal relatedness and individualization; Bion (1959) who described three kinds of basic assumption groups, dependency, fight-flight and the pairing group; Day (1967) who found groups passed through stages of fantasied familiarity, transient victimization, more focused victimization, exaggerated perfect unity and finally individualization; and Kissen (1976) who also included these ingredients.

An early stage of anxiety over the new experience of being in a group, a stage which includes a dependence-independence conflict and a struggle for power or "fight-flight stage," was mentioned by Bion (1959). A stage of group-system formation or "condencer phenomenon," was described by Foulkes and Anthony (1965), a period of polarization or division, and finally a reuniting or reintegrating, culminating in termination.

Psychoanalysis in groups, however, is a totally open ended approach unlike a laboratory or time limited group. People join and leave as they are ready not as part of a whole group readiness phenomenon. The authors believe if the individual in any way goes through stages in groups by the nature of his individuality these stages will occur for each person at different times, based on when he or she joined, how strong his or her ego was to begin with and his or her personal rate of progress. Furthermore, as in psychoanalysis per se, these phases of therapy are based on individual dynamics, ego strength and individual rate of growth. It is like an illustration often given a patient at the beginning of treatment when he or she asks how long it will take: "If someone asked me how long it would take them to get to any location in the city, I would tell him, it depends on where you want to go and how fast a walker you are." For an entire group to go through therapy at the same pace, some would have to walk too fast for others, some too slow, and where they all end up would have to be a compromise.

Additionally, some phases, including some cited above for a group, the authors would not advocate any patient going through. They would, in fact, be part of what has been called irrational psychotherapy (Wolf and Schwartz, 1958, 1959). A stage in group therapy where boundaries between individuals dissolve, to reform later prior to termination, is irrational. The individual at no point should lose his ego with the hope of developing a stronger self later. The ego a patient brings to group can be built on and need not be temporarily dissolved. There are therapists who believe a patient must go through a treatment induced psychosis to come out adjusted at the other end of the tunnel, but that a patient must go through a group therapy induced identity loss is, to us, fallacious and inappropriate.

In psychoanalysis in groups, the group is self-perpetuating. Although there is transplanting of patients, the groups do not entirely disband as a rule. Patients may join and leave.

SUMMARY

The authors of this paper are just as eager as the group dynamists to create a climate in the therapeutic group which is supportive to the reconstructive treatment of the individual but it has been our clinical experience that the most appropriate way to achieve this end is by sponsoring the individual growth of each member's creative ego. This does not mean that we conduct individual analytic groups, but rather that we support interpersonal freedom of expression, of fantasy, association, thoughts, feelings, dreams, ideation, and the analysis and working through of transferences. This does not lead to narcissism but to the development of a realistic self-love and complementary appreciation of the expanding ego of the others.

REFERENCES

Anthony, E. James The History of Group Psychotherapy in Comprehensive Group Psychotherapy, Edited by Harold I. Kaplan and Benjamin J. Sadock, Williams and Wilkins, Publishers, Baltimore, 1971.

Bennis, W. G. and Shepard, H. A. A theory of group development. *Human Relations* 9, 415-437. 1956.

Bion, W. R. *Experiences in groups* Basic Books, New York. 1959.

Day, M. The Natural history of training groups. *International Journal of Group Psychotherapy,* 17, 436-446. 1967.

Foulkes, S. H. and Anthoney, E. J. *Group psychotherapy: The psychoanalytic approach.* Penguin Books, Baltimore, Md.,

Kissen, M. Some dynamic processes observed during an unstructured group laboratory experience in *From Group Dynamics to Group Psychoanalysis,* Washington, D.C. Halsted Press, 51-64, 1976.

Kutash, I. L. and Schlesinger, L. B. *Handbook on Stress and Anxiety,* Jossey-Bass Publishers, San Francisco, 1980.

Kutash, I. L. and Wolf, A. Recent Advances in Psychoanalysis in Groups, *Comprehensive Group Psychotherapy II,* Williams and Wilkins, Publishers, Baltimore 1982.

Martin, E. A. Jr. and Hill, W. F. Toward a theory of group development: six phases of therapy group development. *International Journal of Group Psychotherapy* 7, 20-30, 1957.

Nattland, Candice, Unpublished paper for Introduction to Group Psychotherapy Course, Graduate School of Applied and Professional Psychology, Rutgers University 1983.

Wolf, A. The Psychoanalysis in Groups. *Am. J. Psychother.* 3:525-558, 1949 4:16-50, 1950.

Wolf, A. Psychoanalysis in groups in Comprehensive Group Psychotherapy II, Edited by Harold I. Kaplan and Benjamin J. Sadock, Williams and Wilkins, Publishers, Baltimore 1980.

Wolf, A. and Kutash, I. L. Book Review of Psychoanalytic Group Dynamics edited by Saul Sheidlinger, Ph.D. in *Journal of the American Academy of Psychoanalysis,* Vol. 10, 4, 632-635, 1982.

Wolf, A. and Schwartz, E. K. Irrational psychotherapy: an appeal to unreason, *American Journal of Psychotherapy* 12, 300-315, 508-521, 744-759, 1958 13:383-400, 1959.

Wolf, A. and Schwartz, E. K. *Psychoanalysis in Groups,* Grune and Stratton, New York 1962

The Analyst Visits the Classroom: An Attempt to Resolve Inhibitions

Polly Condit

Ever since Freud, analysts have been concerned with how psychoanalysis can be applied to other fields of knowledge. Every analyst believes that psychoanalytic theory has made significant contributions to many of the social sciences besides psychology, such as anthropology, history, and education. And yet, we don't often go abroad and take our knowledge and expertise into nonanalytic environments. This paper is an attempt to discuss my experience when I overcame some of my inhibitions and ventured forth.

This experience was sparked by my eight-year-old daughter who came home from school one day and told me that her class was studying careers and parents were invited to come and talk about their jobs. After some initial reluctance (it would be hard to talk about psychoanalysis to a class of second-graders) and with much urging from my eager child, I agreed and made a date with the teacher.

My experience in that classroom led me to explore some of my feelings as I moved out of the consultation room into the world and, in addition, it helped me to develop some ideas about the applicability of psychoanalysis to the emotional education of children.

Perhaps nowhere has psychoanalysis had such an effect as on the way we raise our children. Modern psychological and particularly, psychoanalytic understanding of children has profoundly influenced, in fact defined, every aspect of child-rearing. Our knowledge of children's cognitive, perceptual, physical and emotional development at each stage of their growth has enabled us to provide them with an environment most conducive to encouraging their optimal development at each age.

On numerous occasions Freud referred to the impact of education on the emotional development of children. (By education, he meant their entire upbringing, not just formal schooling). He stated (1933) that possibly the most important contribution psychoanalysis could make was to influence our methods in raising future generations. Today, every aspect of child-rearing from reducing trauma at birth to understanding the pains of adolescence owes its beginnings to psychoanalytic knowledge of children developed from Freud's time on.

The importance of school as an integral and vital part of the child's life and, therefore, of his emotional well-being, has been discussed by a number of writers. Fenichel (1945) wrote of the socializing function of schools. The school, as a social institution, plays an important part in developing certain ways of thinking, feeling, and behaving which are necessary if children in any given society are to function in their existing social order. Schools accomplish this by encouraging some kinds of behavior and discouraging others, helping the child find new outlets for his energies when his wishes are frustrated, and providing "good" examples (the teacher) for the child to model himself after.

Anna Freud (1976) discussed the extent to which education has been changed by understanding the child's psychosexual development, the growth of his ego functions and his view of the world as influenced by his drives, defenses and fantasies. Educators have been able to understand how the child experiences school and how he learns at various ages by understanding his inner experience of himself and his environment. Curricula are now developed not just with an eye towards what the child needs to know to make his way in the world but also designed to capitalize on the child's innate push towards exploring himself and his world. His natural curiosity, creativity and ego growth can be tapped and used to advantage in helping him to learn.

Rose Edgcumbe (1975) describes how school is the major contribution of the environment, outside of the parents, to the child's development. School opens up new horizons. Besides the teaching of facts and academic skills, developing intellectual capacities, and the passing along of our culture, school also contributes to enlarging the child's ability to cope with the world by providing a place where he learns to relate, cooperate and work with others. He puts his energies into goal-directed activities, learns to behave constructively and increases his capacities to use his interests and abilities in gratifying ways. All of this he does not alone but in conjunction with teachers and fellow students.

Melanie Klein (1937) views school as a place where the child can have new experiences in relationships outside of the family. He has an opportunity to redo earlier conflicted relationships with parents and siblings. He can experience love, hate, jealousy and competitiveness with less intensity and conflict with his classmates and teachers than with his original family.

It is clear that the classroom, in fact the school as a whole, is a larger, somewhat modified version of the child's nuclear family and a microcosm of the larger world into which he will be going. Among the many things the child must learn as he grows up is how to handle his feelings in ways which are not destructive to himself or to others. He must learn not to strike out in anger but to "make up" after a quarrel, to say the appropriate thing at the right time and not to ventilate his feelings indiscriminately.

But what does he do with all that he feels? How does he learn to understand his feelings? How can he learn to give expression to them without hurting someone else? How can he deal with feelings so that they do not find expression in somatic symptoms? So that he does not stifle his creativity and ability to learn? So that he does not have to suffer from an excess of guilt, fear, or sadness? Children do learn at home and at school to "behave" and to perform a myriad of tasks. But little attention is devoted to helping a child understand his inner life—that complex world of feeling and fantasy which makes each of us who we are.

Edgcumbe (1975) describes the importance of verbalization in helping a child to understand and use his world, whether in therapy or in the classroom.

> Whether the aim is to help the child get the most out of what the environment has to offer, or whether it is to help him understand his inner world, verbalization is the main tool in clarifying and making sense of experiences for the child, in helping him to think rather than act, and in establishing two-way communication with other people. (p. 147)

Anna Freud (1975) in her nursery school at the Hampstead Clinic used the "talking circle" in which children were encouraged to talk to their teachers and classmates about their experiences and feelings. This technique was designed to help children with delayed or inadequate verbal skills due to cultural factors or emotional deprivation. She found that in the talking circle these children rapidly developed their ability to use language to express wishes and ideas.

Nursery education today is very attuned to the emotional needs of the young child, including his need to be able to say what he needs and wants. But it seems not much attention is given to the child's emotional life once he enters elementary school. Spotnitz (1961) discussed the possibility of utilizing the school in the child's emotional upbringing and has suggested that schools provide "emotional training." He states that just as schools took over the intellectual training of children when it became too complicated for parents, so should schools now take responsibility for the emotional training of youngsters. He feels that emotional education should not be left entirely to parents because of almost inevitable failings on their part.

The rationale for emotional education need not be the inability of parents to do the job; rather, there are some important elements in both the school setting itself and in the school-age child's interests and abilities that offer important opportunities for enriching what is learned at home. Here we are not referring to group therapy in schools but to measures that would help children learn how to understand and handle their feelings.

The remaining part of this paper will describe my experience with the children of my daughter's second-grade class.

I gave some thought to how I would describe my work to the children and how to engage them in some way that would be interesting and stimulating. I prepared some notes, with lots of questions and many ready answers, in case I should face a class of silent children. I wanted to talk about therapy in a way that would have some meaning for them. I remembered trying to communicate this to my child patients in our first sessions and how, gradually, as the child and I made contact, his awareness of what therapy is all about developed. Then I decided that instead of worrying so much about imparting some knowledge of therapy, I would draw upon my previous experiences as a child therapist and encourage these children to talk about their feelings.

As I walked into the classroom I found that another second-grade class had been invited to attend so I had over fifty children in front of me. I told them I was a psychotherapist and asked if anyone knew what that was. Several eager hands went up with comments such as "Someone you talk to about your problems" and "Someone you tell your feelings to"—obviously sophisticated children probably in therapy themselves. The children all laughed when I said some kids have called me a "talking doctor" and that I helped people with hurt feelings rather than hurt bodies.

I then asked the children to name as many different feelings as they could—good feelings as well as bad feelings—and was surprised by the wide and sophisticated range of feelings that were called out, one after another. "Joyful," "excited," "worried," and "mean" were a few that stand out in my mind.

I began to sense a certain excitement in the room. The idea of talking about feelings was obviously very stimulating to these children.

I next asked them to tell me what kinds of things they thought children worried about. Again I was very impressed with their eagerness to talk about feelings, fantasies and conflicts. Hands shot up all over the room. Not surprising with this age group, there were lots of worries about parents getting divorced. School problems (not getting work done), getting bad marks, getting into trouble with the teacher, were a big concern as well. I said that children, and sometimes grownups too, get themselves into trouble and don't know why. A little girl called out, "Yeah, me!"

Brief encouragement from me led into another barrage of statements about fights with siblings and friends, arguments with parents, and scary dreams. Dreams were a big subject and when I said that the monster that chases you at night is the mad feeling you had during the day, there was laughter and more comments about feeling angry.

By this time the words were tumbling out. I thought that we should talk also about good feelings. (Maybe I was feeling a little anxious about the intensity and eagerness with which these children wanted to talk about their problems).

They somewhat dutifully, at this point, named a number of items that children feel good about but obviously their hearts were not in it—they wanted to go back to more pressing concerns. We then talked about grownups. I asked what kinds of things they thought grownups worried about. The response: jobs, fighting and paying taxes. I talked briefly about how grownups worry about their jobs just as children worry about school. They were delighted when I said that grownups were a lot like kids—they can feel jealous of their brothers and sisters too.

I then talked about what you can do about your hurt or worried feelings. A child immediately suggested that you can talk to someone. When I asked if any child there ever got so mad he threw something, they suggested that they could ride their bike very fast or hit something or someone. Everyone nodded in agreement. One boy said that when his parents are angry at someone, they will yell at him. I said that parents when they're angry sometimes pick on children just as children sometimes pick on younger sisters or brothers. More laughter.

I wanted, at this point, to try briefly to bring therapy into the discussion and to sum up, since it was near the end of my scheduled time. I said that sometimes when hurt feelings do not go away, and when nobody seems to understand or to be able to help, a person might go to see a therapist. Sometimes children go, sometimes teenagers, sometimes mommies and daddies, or whole families. When you talk to a therapist you can say anything you want to and no one tells you to be quiet or "that's not nice." You can say things you never said to anyone before. You and the therapist will try to understand why you feel the way you do and how you can feel better. Then I asked for any questions.

Almost every hand in the room went up. I glanced at the two teachers, who said to go on—don't worry about time. What happened next is what really precipitated the writing of this article. As I began to call on the children, one after another, I was deeply moved and somewhat overwhelmed by the urgency and intensity of their responses. A few children had "technical" questions such as "How many times did you go to therapy?" "How long does it take to become a therapist?" "If you know how to help people, why do you need to go to therapy yourself?" But the rest of the questions and statements were obviously coming from very personal concerns. Some children were more pressing in their demands to talk—often bringing up the same issue over and over. The overriding concern in the room was divorce. Why parents get divorced, what happens to the kids, "What if neither my mommy nor my daddy wants me?" which parent should get the child, fears of moving, of fighting and of rejection. One boy asked (a modern, enlightened child), "My parents go to therapy and what if the therapist tells them that they have to get divorced?" The children asked how they could stop their parents from fighting, did parents ever get back together, who decides where the child will live—"What if my brother wants to go with daddy and I want to stay with mommy?" "Can kids ever get a new family?"

The talk went on and on. Each statement seemed to stimulate

another child to say something. I responded each time, if I could, with brief comments, trying to relate to the child's feeling and to allay some anxiety. An hour passed very quickly and we stopped only because the final school bell rang.

The teachers told me they wished that they had taped our discussion. Both teachers were quite psychologically minded, in tune with some of the children's difficulties. They had expected their bright and verbal children to speak up. But neither expected the intensity of feeling that was generated in the room.

I said to the teachers I thought it was fortunate that some time, like this, to talk about the everyday concerns that face all children was not built into the curriculum. One teacher said that she tried occasionally to have class discussions about feelings and behavior but she felt the pressure of time. So much material had to be covered that almost every moment was accounted for. I thought of how we work so hard to educate our children. These children get a great deal of attention paid to developing their academic skills and intellectual capacities and considerably less time spent on artistic creativity and physical and social development. But no time really is allotted to educating and developing the child's ability to cope with the conflicts and concerns that are so much a part of every child and will affect him so much as he grows up. We provide therapy for children when they behave in such a way that makes us see they are not managing their feelings well. But we officially ignore, the rest of the time, the child's inner life—his fears, conflicts, wishes and questions concerning his life.

In junior and senior high school some attention is paid to the teenager's emerging concerns about his place in the world through such courses as sex and family life education. But our younger children need time to talk too.

The elementary school years encompass a period of tremendous ego growth in the child. Far from being a quiet time, the latency stage of a child's development is when the youngster begins to move away from his attachment to his family into the outside social world, pursuing in the process all kinds of intellectual, social and emotional goals. Anna Freud (1965) in her developmental scheme defined this period as moving from "egocentricity to companionship." The child is no longer so enveloped in his intense feelings and preoccupations with Mommy and Daddy but becomes involved in complicated individual and group relationships with peers and identifies with other important adults in his life.

Sarnoff (1976) describes the latency child as moving from fantasy based on affective attachment to family to a reality most importantly influenced by peers and experiences gained outside of the family. The child now has opportunities to modify and develop new patterns of behavior. He is very concerned about making ethical decisions and working out problems with his friends. Blos (1962) stresses the child's interest in and assimilation of values, his emerging social awareness and his increased capacity for verbalization.

The choice of reading material shown by the grade school child illustrates many of the issues with which he is struggling. He no longer is so interested in fantasies, fairy tales or animal-people stories. He prefers to read about people solving their problems, biographies and adventure stories. He chooses books about "real" people dealing with human dilemmas. He wants to know how others think and feel, how they make decisions and what they choose to do.

As I think back on my group of second-graders, I feel that we are missing something essential in the education of our children. A part of every child's school week should be a chance to talk and share with others his worries, fears, joys and doubts. He should have an opportunity to talk about things that are not dealt with, except maybe in passing, during the rest of his day. He should be given a chance to explore his inner life and to relate these feelings to his life in the outer world. We have an opportune time and place in which we could give children skills and understanding that would serve them in good stead for the rest of their lives. Both the school setting and the developmental tasks of the school-age child, as we have seen, provide a rich atmosphere for helping children to learn about themselves. The social function and structure of the school, the child's identification with his teachers and friends, his concerns with building relationships and his capacity to put his ideas into words are all important elements in helping him to grow through group discussions.

The leader of the group need not be a psychoanalyst. In fact, it is especially important that the teacher lead the discussions. As a major role model for the children, she needs to give permission for them to talk freely and to listen to them with empathy. She must be understanding, attuned to the meanings of the children's concerns and feel comfortable with her own feelings, which are bound to be aroused as the children talk. Available psychoanalytic consultation would be very helpful. Being allowed to express feelings openly, to hear that others have similar thoughts, to exchange ideas about what to do about problems and to feel the support and concern of teacher and classmates will go a long way towards helping a child handle feelings more effectively. Children can better cope with vague anxieties by putting them into words and then, through talking, feel less frightened and guilty about their thoughts. They can learn that it's not so bad to feel mean or jealous. They can discharge energy that might have gone into a destructive act by sharing their unacceptable wishes with their friends. They can learn to be more tolerant of themselves and others, perhaps even to laugh at things that didn't seem so funny before.

When I think of the topics that came up in my brief time in the classroom, the universality of the children's concerns was striking to me. They were worried about the things we all worry about—anger, work problems, jealousy, scary thoughts. Even the major theme of the day, divorce, had many universal elements in it. These children were not just thinking about divorce, although that is a pressing worry for all children today, whether or not their own parents are getting divorced. I think that the theme of divorce allowed these children to express many questions about themselves and their parents including, "How do each of my parents feel about me and how do I feel about them?" This is part of coming to terms with one's place in the family, with all the loving and angry feelings toward those who are closest.

Psychoanalysis can be applied to the classroom in another, less formalized way than scheduled discussions. All children have feelings and fantasies when they perform mathematics, read history or study science. The teacher who is sensitized to the children's concerns can discuss sibling rivalry and family changes as the children add and subtract, or grandparents when history is studied, or feelings and moods when the human body is the subject. Less separation between emotional experience and academic learning would enhance both the child's ability to learn and his ability to use his feelings in a creative way.

My experience of going into the classroom proved enormously enriching for me. My attempt at creatively using my interest and abilities ouside of my usual milieu led me to these thoughts about how we might enrich the experiences of our children. We know that talking about ourselves and listening to others helps us to feel less frightened, less ashamed and less angry. Perhaps if we give children the same chance to do this, not just at home but in school, where so much of their development is occurring, they would grow up less frightened of their feelings and more able to love and share with others.

BIBLIOGRAPHY

Blos, Peter, *On Adolescence: A Psychoanalytic Interpretation,* New York, Free Press, 1962.

Edgcumbe, Rose, "The Border Between Therapy and Education," *Studies in Child Psychoanalysis: Pure and Applied,* Monograph Series of the Psychoanalytic Study of the Child, New Haven, Yale University Press, 1975.

Fenichel, Otto, "The Means of Education," *The Psychoanalytic Study of the Child,* Vol. I., 1945.

Freud, Anna, *Normality and Pathology in Childhood,* New York, International Universities Press, 1965.

————, *Psychoanalytic Psychology of Normal Development,* The Writing of Anna Freud, Vol. VIII, New York, International Universities Press, 1975.

————, "The Nursery School of the Hempstead Child-Therapy Clinic," *Studies in Child Psychoanalysis: Pure and Applied,* New Haven, Yale University Press, 1976.

Freud, Sigmund, New Introductory Lectures on Psychoanalysis, Lecture XXXIV, Standard Edition, Vol. XXII, London, The Hogarth Press, 1933.

Klein, Melanie, "Love, Guilt, and Reparation," *Love, Guilt and Reparation and Other Works, 1921-1945,* New York, Dell Publishing Co., 1937.

Sarnoff, Charles, *Latency,* New York, Jason Aronson, Inc., 1976.

Spotnitz, Hyman, *The Couch and the Circle,* New York, Alfred A. Knopf., 1961.

"The Wish Not to Know": A Fool Cannot Be Blamed for His Actions

Robert C. Lane
Robert S. Storch

This paper will be concerned mainly with how drive and trauma, particularly primal scene trauma, influence the wish not to know. Although the authors' position is in agreement with A. Freud (1967), Herman and Lane (1979) and H. Blum (1974, 1979), among others who point out that the primal scene is but one part of a constellation of factors that contribute to trauma resulting in pathogenicity, they believe that drive theory has not received sufficient attention in the more recent literature. In order to accomplish their mission, the authors revisit a number of the classic writings in the field.

S. Freud (1910) in his seminal paper on psychogenic visual disturbance implied the equation that the wish not to see was the equivalent of the wish not to know. Certain ideas related to seeing (knowing) had to be segregated from consciousness or repressed because they had ". . . come into opposition with other more powerful ideas," (p. 108). The paper is replete with expressions like, "Conflict of interests," "contradiction of ideas," "battle of Instincts." Freud says:

> If the sexual component instinct which makes use of sight—the sexual 'lust of the eye'—has drawn down upon itself, through its exorbitant demands, some retaliatory measure from the side of the ego-instincts, so that the ideas which represent the content of its strivings are subjected to repression and withheld from consciousness, the general relation of the eye and the

faculty of vision to the ego and to consciousness is radically disturbed. The ego has lost control of the organ, which now becomes solely the instrument of the repressed sexual impulse. (1910, p. 110)

Thus, the talion principle acts in a way to bring about an inhibition of seeing or looking in the patient. Freud brings out the dual function of the eye: to perceive one's environment for the preservation of life and the seeking of erotic gratification. The "outbreak of psychogenic visual disturbance" is the result of repression of the sexual component instinct, scoptophilia, which ". . . must be suppressed, restrained, transmuted, directed toward loftier goals, for civilized psychical achievement to take place" (p. 109).

Abraham (1913), commenting on Freud's paper, felt that the instance of hysterical blindness was indeed rare and addressed himself to a number of other psychogenic problems related to restrictions and transformations of the scoptophilic instinct. He states:

> What I want to bring forward is the fact that in quite a number of instances the pleasure the child has derived at night from watching its parents and listening to them has led to an oversensitiveness both to light and to sound. (p. 183)

He goes on to say, "Such impressions fixate the scoptophilic instinct on the parents in an unusual degree, so that later efforts to detach it from them are doomed to failure" (p. 193). The sensitiveness of the eyes to light even when exposed for a short time, and the need to protect the eyes from sunlight, daylight or artificial light, suggest that the eyes have seen or looked at something forbidden. The viewer doesn't want to know or want others to know the content of what has been seen or looked at. What has been seen could be the primal scene, the mother's nude body, especially her genitals, or other forbidden sights. The sexual pleasure in looking (knowing) is associated with being discovered by the father's ever-watchful, all powerful omniscient eye which might render the looker blind (castrated).

Abraham described a patient subject to bizarre body vibrations and twitching attacks on the couch. She had ". . . a repressed and incestuously fixated pleasure in looking which was directed on to her father and his body" (p. 192). These bizarre attacks were a repetition of a primal scene she had witnessed in early childhood.

She displayed ". . . an avoidance of all sexual looking and knowledge" (p. 193) which extended to seeing in general. This included ". . . an anxious avoidance of reading anything that might give her any enlightenment on love and sexual passion" (p. 193). Thus, in 1913 Abraham had pointed out a relationship between the primal scene, its reliving in a motoric symptom, and the avoidance of all sexual looking and knowing, including reading.

Fenichel (1937) writes: "In the unconscious, to look at an object may mean various things, the most noteworthy of which are as follows: to devour the object looked at, to grow like it (be forced to imitate it) or, conversely, to force it to grow like oneself" (p. 376). He indicated that when someone gazes intently at an object (like a book) we say he "devours it with his eyes." Fenichel observes that when a child has witnessed the primal scene ". . . he identifies himself with that which he sees" (p. 375), and the relationship between looking and identification may have important consequences during his lifetime.

In 1945, Fenichel expanded his views on the inhibition of sexual curiosity and the repression of scoptophilia. He held the following view:

A repression of sexual curiosity may block the normal interest in knowing and thinking. Often the inhibited sexual curiosity corresponds to an intense unconscious scoptophilia or stands in intimate relationship to sadistic impulses; the consequent "stupidity" may represent simultaneously an obedience to and a rebellion against the parents from whom the patient had suffered frustrations of his curiosity. (p. 181)

While Freud (1910) and Abraham (1913) anticipate the extensive later literature concerning the relationship between early visual and auditory experience and reading, it remained for Melanie Klein to give its most powerful statement. She writes:

J. Strachey (1930) has shown that reading has the unconscious significance of taking knowledge out of the mother's body, and that the fear of robbing her is an important factor for inhibitions in reading. I should like to add that it is essential for a favourable development of the desire for knowledge that the mother's body should be felt to be well and unharmed. It represents in the unconscious the treasure-house of everything desirable which can only be got from there; therefore if it is not destroyed, not so much in danger and therefore not too dangerous itself, the wish to take food for the mind from it can more easily be carried out. (1931, p. 241)

She adds that the reduction of a person's inhibition, of really knowing about the inside of his own body, at the same time leads to a deeper understanding and better control of his own mental processes, he can then clear up and bring order to his own mind. The first results in a greater capacity to take in knowledge; the second entails a better ability to work over, organize and correlate the knowledge obtained, and also to give it out again (1931, p. 244).

This distinction between receptive and integrative disability seems to us a very important one.

Jarvis (1958) notes that her patients had an avoidance of looking and dreaded any encounter of the eye and the printed word for fear of going blind or being castrated. They were unable to look at books, the eye being a symbolic penis that penetrates the book which symbolizes the female genital, the dangerous mother and teacher. The avoidance of looking represents a scoptophilic and not a visual problem. Fenichel (1937) states, ''. . . exhibitionists are always active scoptophilics as well,'' (p. 377), a point elaborated by Jarvis (1958), Allen et al. (1967). Allen feels there is ''. . . at least one vivid traumatic incident in the phallic or latency period in which childhood voyeurism or exhibitionism was severely reproved by the mother with her threat of loss of love'' (p. 547).

E. Blum (1926) in a paper on examination anxiety points out that this symptom is also associated with the wish not to know or a denial of knowledge. To him, the search and desire for knowledge is a search for the penis, a search to answer infantile sexual inquiries. The child attributes omnipotence to the parents who, he feels, can read his mind, know his secret thoughts, find out the nature of his curiosity, particularly about the primal scene, and punish him with castration or loss of love. The test becomes the vehicle of discovery of forbidden thoughts, feelings, wishes and actions. The omnipotence of the authority objects is displaced on to the test and the examiner who will discover all the secret wishes. Blum saw a relationship between looking, knowing, eating and examination anxiety. Abraham (1924, p. 404) had pointed out that the receptive function in eating was the prototype for all later intellectual understanding and that disturbances in pleasure in the oral phase led to disturbances in the intellectual sphere. The relationship between difficulty in oral intake and the intake of knowledge was also suggested by Glover (1925), Bornstein (1930), Strachey (1930), Fenichel (1937), Schmideberg (1938), Blanchard (1946), E. Klein (1949), Pearson (1952), Hellman (1954), and others.

Schmideberg elaborated on the remarks of Abraham. She pointed to the link between the wish to know (take in) everything and omnipotence. By knowing one is omnipotent, this omnipotence leads to independence of the parents. The wish not to know suggests one's lost omnipotence, which the mother possesses, and one's dependence on her. Schmideberg summarizes her position:

> I found that the most powerful factors inhibiting oral-intellectual ingestion were: Fear of the envy of others corresponding in intensity to one's own envy of their possessions, fear of one's sadism (of destroying food, damaging knowledge, depriving others of it by one's incompetence, that is, sadism) and further numerous incorporation anxieties. An additional motive of importance emphasized by various writers is oral defiance; a refusal to take in knowledge because as a child one did not obtain it at the time or in the way or as fully as one wished. (1938, p. 20)

If we examine the literature dealt with thus far, we cannot avoid noticing the frequency with which primal scene exposure occurs in the discussion of the wish not to know. There are a host of recent papers on primal scene including the Kris Study Group Report (1969), Esman (1973), Myers (1973, 1979), H. Blum (1974, 1979), Isay (1975, 1978), Arlow (1978, 1980). A number of these papers indicate a possible relationship between the primal scene, the wish not to know and learning problems. Freud, in the case of the Wolf-Man (1918), felt that a single exposure was traumatic and concluded that witnessing the primal scene would have a damaging effect on the child. H. Blum (1974) offers other possibilities for the Wolf-Man's traumatization. Esman reviews the literature on primal scene up to 1973, including all of Freud's writings on the subject. He says in response to the many different types of pathology attributed to the primal scene, "One is moved to wonder whether we are here confronted by one of those situations in which a theory, by explaining everything, succeeds in explaining nothing" (p. 65). Blum summarizes the currently held view:

The primal scene . . . must be evaluated in terms of its actual effects at the time of the experience, the child's ego state and development, and the total psychic situation, including the reaction of the parents at the time and the influence of earlier and later developmental phases and experiences upon each other. The nature of the trauma also depends upon the degree of the child's ego maturity, fantasy life, and ego strength, and the revival of old conflicts and traumata versus the capacity for meeting developmental challenge and mastery of trauma. (1979, p. 39)

Myers reviews the literature on chronic primal scene exposure and concludes ". . . that chronic primal scene exposure within our cultural milieu is traumatic and pathogenic" (1979, p. 21). Such repeated exposures can lead to the need to repress, and pathology concerning the ability to see and to know. He points out that all ten patients in his study exhibited learning difficulties.

One expression of the wish not to know is playing dumb or exhibiting a make-believe stupidity. Papers by Jones (1910), Landauer (1929), Bornstein (1930), Bergler (1932), Oberndorf (1939), Mahler (1942), Hellman (1954), Sprince (1967), and Berger and Kennedy (1975) all deal with this.

This symptom of innocence and ignorance has been referred to by many names in literature including pseudodebility, pseudostupidity, pseudoimbecility and pseudobackwardness. All of the above imply a lack of knowledge of sexual matters. A number of these papers discuss the role of parents, particularly the mother, in the child's development of a learning inhibition: Mahler (1942), Staver (1953), Hellman (1954), Buxbaum (1964), Sprince (1967), A. Freud (1975), Berger and Kennedy (1975), Kaye (1982). Jones said in 1910:

When a mother chats with her intimate friends over various private topics, frequently the child will resort to the strongest devices in order to stay in the room and listen to the conversation. Then when someone remarks him, and by her look insinuates a doubt as to the propriety of conversing in his presence, he will interrupt his innocent crooning over his toys and indulge in exaggeratedly foolish antics, to disarm, as it were, the suspicions of the company by convincing them of his thorough simplemindedness and innocence. (p. 151)

Mahler's paper (1942) attempts to demonstrate that the magic cap the child uses ". . . as a means of restoring and maintaining a secret libidinous rapport within the family" (p. 4) is "stupidity." The pseudostupidity of these children permitted them ". . . to participate in the sexual life of parents and other adults to an amazingly unlimited extent which overtly expressed would be strictly and definitely forbidden" (p. 4). These children do not renounce sexual gratification and maintain their omnipotence through the use of their magic cap of stupidity.

Esman, commenting on Mahler's paper, says:

> Mahler (1942) attributes the syndrome of pseudostupidity in part to a defensive response to primal scene observation ("I didn't see it, I don't know anything about it, but I can still be around to watch") but she adduces a number of other determinants as well, including the child's compliance to the mother's wish for him to be stupid. (1973, p. 58)

Arlow uses Mahler's findings as an example of an elaboration of the primal scene. He writes:

> Mahler was able to trace a form of make believe stupidity to the child's need to remain unknowing in the primal-scene situation. By acting as if he were ignorant, the child fends off the danger of provoking his parent's wrath and punishment and at the same time permits the exciting activity to continue without interruption. Such feigned ignorance may involve other areas of ego functioning, sometimes culminating in a clinical picture resembling genuine mental retardation. (1980, p. 520)

The relevance of this work is pointed out by Fenichel when he links debility to resistance. He comments on intellectual inhibitions and how they are used in the analytic hour and says:

> The existence of the mechanism of intellectual inhibition can be studied in every analytic hour marked by resistance. Every intellect begins to show weakness when affective motives are working against it. Analysts talk jokingly of "slight" dementia by resistance. (1945, p. 180)

In a case Mahler describes, an eighteen-year-old boy whose curiosity was restricted, resolved his problem by transforming curiosity into voyeurism, secretly creeping around and spying on everyone. He was permitted in the bathroom when his mother was bathing and even in his brother's marital bedroom during sexual preliminaries. By appearing ignorant, absent-minded and innocent, he both warded off voyeurism and at the same time satisfied his very strong voyeuristic inclinations. The pseudostupidity of the child is reinforced by parents and siblings who wish the child to remain innocent because of their own unconscious needs. Mutual sexual desires are gratified on a pre-verbal level and both child and mother continue to maintain a "gratifying affective communication" despite the child's chronological growth. Mahler says, "In all these conflict situations between children and parents we are struck again and again by the intuitive accuracy with which children are able to detect the weakest spots in their parents, and how often they succeed in gaining entrance and seducing the parents to respond in the old affective way" (1942, p. 6). Another case described by Mahler concerned chronic forgetting in a thirteen-year-old boy. Each time he revealed one of his fantasies, there was an intensification of his forgetting (a severe restriction of his ego). Kestenberg (1972) in her paper, "How Children Remember and Parents Forget," discusses the influence of parents on remembering and forgetting, parents' need for a child not to remember, and certain patients' need to get "permission" from their parents before they can accept a reconstruction.

Anna Freud and Berger and Kennedy agree with Mahler, emphasizing that these intellectually inhibited children ". . . do not wish to understand, to know, to see; and their defensive ignorance pertains especially to sexual matters" (1975, p. 281). The sexual matters are felt to be part of a family secret involving the child as an observer or participant in the sexual activities of parents or close relatives, causing much guilt and conflict. The stupidity of the child in these cases is maintained and even encouraged by parents who unconsciously need a particular child to remain "not knowing" and the child who is seeking to preserve parental love conforms to their demands (p. 305). Berger and Kennedy state:

> The emphasis in all these papers is on the impairment of the children's ego functions and on the inhibition of curiosity and scoptophilia which results from the children's unconscious collusion with their mothers in the need not to know the parental secrets. (p. 281)

Hellman (1954) in a paper on three mothers of children with severe intellectual inhibitions (one couldn't read or write, a second couldn't spell a three-letter word, while the third was a case of pseudoimbecility) points out the strong bond between these mothers and their learning disordered children and the effects of the mother's use of denial and lying about her activities on her child's pathology. The child was not permitted to show any independent activity, any curiosity concerning the mother's affairs, or any criticism of the mother. Everything had to be kept in and remain secret. The mother needed to deny the impact of her secrets on her child. Close attachment to any object other than the mother, including the father, was forbidden. These mothers need to keep the child "passive and stupid" for as soon as they experience the child's growth and movement away from them, they experience intolerable anxiety. The child in turn cannot move away from or against the mother, as this would expose them, as well as the mother, to dangers. Safety prevails "only in unity with mother." At the same time, the child is rewarded for illness, weakness and fears with sympathy, nursing, comfort, food, kisses and cuddling.

Stavers (1953) studied seventeen cases of intellectual retardation and concluded that in each case the mother had some unconscious need for the child not to learn. Berger and Kennedy (1975) agree that the mothers need to keep their children "passive and stupid" but feel the child's compliance has deeper motives than the need to preserve secrets. They found that the mothers were ambivalent to their pseudobackward children and needed to denigrate them. Fathers shared and reinforced the negative aspect of the mothers' ambivalence. Several of the mothers fantasized they would produce a damaged child, inadequate, of limited intelligence and physical growth. These mothers were said to use the child as a "vehicle" onto which they projected unwanted aspects of their own poor self-images (stupidity, castration), thus perpetuating in relationship to the child the denigration the mother herself experienced.

In a more recent paper, Jacobs (1980) addressed the question of personal and family secrets and alliances. The major point of his paper follows:

> Certain secrets, especially those that relate to a parent's romantic and sexual life and that come into awareness during the oedipal and early latency periods, can have as strong an impact on the imagination and on sexual fantasies as actual sexual

stimulation or the witnessing of sexual activity. Not only are voyeuristic impulses, primal scene fantasies, or memories, and oedipal wishes stimulated by awareness of the parent's secret activity, but a stamp of reality is given to the notion of an illicit, secretive relationship. Nor is it only in the case of secrets of a sexual kind that the child's sexual fantasies may be stimulated. The child invariably experiences family secrets in terms of his own secrets, which in part, include secret sexual wishes and masturbatory practices. (p. 33)

It can be implied from the above statement that secrets may act as traumas and have a strong effect on molding the central masturbation fantasy (Laufer, 1976).

After a concentrated review of the extensive literature we can see that "the wish not to know" has many motives, purposes and functions. Included among these are both instinctual material such as primal scene trauma, repressed scoptophilia and sadism, and interactional material such as a wish to remain unknowing, stupid and dependent on an omnipotent symbiotic mother in order to retain her love, a wish to avoid the wrath of an all-seeing omniscient father, and a fear of being envied by others. In every case there appears to be a wish to avoid both sexual and hostile knowledge and a need to maintain family and personal secrets. The wish not to know is at the heart of all resistance, which is the essence of the analytic process.

Before proceeding to our discussion of various illustrations of the wish not to know, mention should be made of the justifiably famous case of Ivan described by Margerie P. Sprince (1967). At age thirteen, Ivan was "backward, lazy, slovenly and lacking in spontaneity." As his analysis progressed, it became clear that these characteristics were an unconsciously contrived facade he had adopted. He came to understand that the major factors in his debility were his effort to "turn off his heat" (sexual knowledge), and avoid responsibility for his actions. As he stated, *sotto voce,* at a particularly poignant moment in therapy: "A fool cannot be blamed for his actions." This phrase sums up what in our view is a major affirmative function of not knowing. We will propose that in addition to the other functions mentioned in the literature, playing the fool or madman serves as an abnegation or denial of responsibility for words and actions, and that the person seeks leave and sanction for his aggressiveness by compromising his credibility with the authorities.

Our first clinical vignette concerns a young man of good intellectual potential whose failures had permeated every aspect of his life. At twenty-three, Alan was very heavily into the drug world. Violent outbreaks towards family and friends prompted his third entry into therapy. Both earlier abortive attempts were with male therapists. He reported that he terminated because the first doctor "did not listen" and because the second appeared so shocked by Alan's history that he "was afraid and left." This time the therapist was a woman, to whom Alan's parents would pay the fee, since he had never been able to hold a job and had no prospects.

His history was a very disordered one. He was the second of two boys, his brother three years older. Both brothers had serious academic and behavioral problems in school, achieving only moderate success in various team sports. Even here there were incessant fights with coaches and teammates. Alan recalls, when being called upon in class, "forgetting all I knew, breaking out in a sweat, my heart pounding and my anxiety almost uncontrollable." He thought of himself as stupid and incapable and took naturally to the more tawdry aspects of the upper middle-class suburban school he attended. Early on, he became involved with drugs and sexual procuring for classmates.

Alan's sexual development was quite precocious. At four years of age, he was "selected" by the neighborhood girls for their favorite game—doctor. Until eight, he was nocturnally enuretic, and at ten he recalls his boy friends' comparing genitals and masturbating. At thirteen, Alan was invited to go to Europe with Carol, a girl he knew, her father and his girl-friend. Significantly, his parents allowed him to go, and he lived with Carol during the entire summer trip. Her father and his girl-friend were in one room, Alan and Carol in the other. Alan was treated to the entire trip, required only to keep Carol "out of her father's hair both day and night." By seventeen, Alan had arranged sex for many of his friends. He also produced drugs for these episodes. At this time Alan had his first experience of impotence and became deeply worried. This eventually passed and he resumed his frenetic activities. Generally he dated "troubled girls" he attempted to rescue from some dire fate—depression, the mafia and such.

It took two years in therapy for Alan to recall and report his first dream: He had stolen a workbench from a neighbor's house, he first dropped it behind a bush, then, after being silently confronted by the owner, picked it up and walked away. His associations emphasized the theft of the workbench (penis) from the house (mother) and the man's (father's) tacit consent to his theft. Two days after the dream, a flood of painful memories came back to him at his session. He recalled that when he was four or five, his mother had begun to walk around nude in front of him and discussed her body parts. He especially remembered her using the term "vagina." He recalls at the time feeling "terribly excited and stunned." Leaving the session, he commented that "a great weight has been lifted from me."

His second dream followed soon thereafter. It depicted a girl he knew who was making love to a man whose face he could not see. His first thoughts were as to why this particular girl appeared, he thought he might identify with her—her helplessness. He recalled a T.V. show where a gynecologist commented about women's anxiety during a gynecological exam becoming so great that they forgot what they wanted to ask the doctor. (A statement of the pseudostupidity with which Alan identifies and replicates). He then mentioned his anger, to this day, when "I catch my mother naked." This led him to recall the always-open parental bedroom door, his often looking in and being aroused, masturbating and/or wetting the bed. Next he recalled head injuries as a toddler and suggested that, like burn victims who sustain head and hand injuries, he may have lost his sense of self and withdrawn in the face of these multiple trauma.

As these deeply repressed memories and fantasies have been recovered, Alan and his therapist have been able to confront the traumatic and overwhelmingly stupifying effects that they had upon him. His equation of all knowledge, progress and development with the readily available, highly-charged but still dangerous sexual knowledge (mother, her genitals, the primal scene), has now been modulated so that he can sort out his sexuality, and hence his capacity to know, from these forbidden matters. He is now working regularly, is back in school, and beginning to date. With his therapist he is very gingerly working at disentangling all the dangerous id material from his legitimate ego functions and mastery. Resistances have been numerous, negative transference frequent, but, through it all, Alan and his therapist have sustained a scrupulous focus upon past trauma and their present transference expressions. They have come to see these as remediable and modifiable facts which can be faced and must be grown beyond. For him, as a castrated woman undergoing a gynecological examination, to *forget his questions* is no longer a viable adaptation. As his therapist remarks: "Since past is but prologue we continue to regard it our tool not our disaster."

Our second example describes a more subtle and delimited instance of pseudostupidity. Whereas virtually all of Alan's ego functioning was impaired by his wish (perhaps need) not to know, Joan has many areas of good functioning. She is a happily married, career woman in her mid-thirties, busily concerned with her high-level professional position. She still tends to have obsessional ruminations concerning trivial aspects of her life, and often remains counterproductively fixed upon such things as what color dress to wear to a conference or what brand of food to buy in the supermarket. Whereas these choices were totally debilitating at earlier stages of her life, they are now merely bothersome and annoying. When called upon to travel to an unfamiliar destination, Joan still tends to become quite flustered. She anticipates that she will have great difficulty making travel plans, deciding what to do when she arrives, and budgeting her time. She "knows" how to read maps and follow directions but becomes quite panicky at the prospect of having to do so.

While Joan has discussed at great length the conflicts and implications of not wanting to have any children, at this stage her decision is a firm one. She understands that her parents' negative attitudes towards her and her femininity are involved but she feels that beyond these "neurotic reasons" there are valid "reality considerations." She mentions children as preoccupying and demanding and, in general, an "inconvenience and nuisance."

Joan grew up on a farm in a small midwestern community. The farm had been set up by her mother's father who, together with his wife, maintained overall control during his lifetime. Their children had married and stayed home with their own families to help work the farm, often building their own houses on the property. This was the case for Joan's mother, who married, built a house and lived there with her husband and children. Joan's father left home when she was fourteen. He had become involved with some kind of scandal in his business, about which Joan is not too clear. She does, though, remember her mother opportunistically using this as an occasion to end what had always been a bad marriage. Most significant to our topic was her mother's reaction to her husband's behavior. She spared no effort to disguise, distort and generally misrepresent what had happened. Her distortion of the event was as much for the extended family as it was for the neighbors. Such mythologizing, "rewriting history" and, in general lying to herself, her family and the community, was characteristic of the mother's behavior. The entire family had always placed a tremendous emphasis on looks and facade, frequently doing extreme violence to accuracy and truth. In any competition between appearance and reality, in Joan's house appearance won hands down.

As we might expect, academic achievement was always given high priority for Joan and her siblings. She did very well in school and the parents were asked to allow her to skip one of the early grades. Joan was very much opposed, but her parents urged her to do it, emphasizing "how good it looked to have someone in the family so honored." While for all the children the facts of their family history were fudged and hazy, the three R's were sharp, clear and implacable.

Increasingly, as she grew up, Joan understandably came to emphasize form over content. She continued to excel in school, but there was a real lack of depth and comprehension about her attainments. It was as if once-over-lightly glibness held priority over any depth of understanding. Unquestionably the prototype for this was Joan's always occupying the room immediately adjacent to her parents. She recalled "seeing things, hearing things," but never developed any thoughts, hypotheses or questions about them. Indeed, despite growing up on the farm she claims that up until college, she had absolutely no knowledge, comprehension or curiosity about sexuality or reproduction. When her younger sisters and brother were born, she neither knew, wondered or asked where they came from. They appeared and, according to Joan's lights, that was all that mattered. She dealt with them.

A current dream she described bespeaks this life-long disinclination "to ask": "I am in a resort of some kind with my husband and a very heavy fog sets in. He wants to go to look for the group we are with. But I tell him it's no use, we will never penetrate the fog and may get lost and wander into a bog, so we stay where we are."

A preferred recent sexual fantasy for Joan has been bondage. She likes to imagine being tied up and ravaged. The fantasies she has about this are that she is then in no way responsible for having sex and any of the gratifications and pleasures are not attributable to her and "plumbing the depths of my own lust." These bondage predilections recall the oft-repeated masturbatory fantasy that she is lying helpless on an operating-room table in a crowded surgical theatre with her hands and feet tied. The surgeon makes an incision from her head to her vagina, baring all of her insides. The turn-on of this fantasy is her helplessness and passivity and the masochistic enjoyment she derives out of the renunciation of responsibility for the entire scene.

All of these issues come together in Joan's current rejection of the idea of motherhood. She has some very basic questions about herself, her femininity and her capacity to bear a child, and in a very literal sense does not wish to risk learning "how it will come out." The bright, urbane, sophisticated professional is a facade she presents very successfully, but she is reluctant to penetrate into the knowledge of whether she is really a woman capable of bearing a healthy normal child.

Ernest Jones (1949) observed that down through history and exemplified in literature, the fool or madman has always occupied a very privileged position. Under the protection (or guise) of his stupidity or madness, he has been able to give voice to sentiments that would not be tolerated in other people. He could speak the most critical calumnies and heresies against the establishment and be dismissed as a fool or deranged, or just plain stupid. His stupidity "neutralized him" in the eyes of the authorities and made him safe and innocuous. Speaking of Hamlet, Jones writes, "His motive in so acting was, by playing the part of a harmless fool, to deceive the King and court as to his projects of revenge, and unobserved to get to know their plans and intentions; in this he admirably succeeded" (1949, p. 164).

This "function of stupidity" provides us with a slightly different slant in our clinical material. Not only does stupidity serve to disguise, placate, protect, and emulate, it serves also to provide impunity from counterattack. The person's critique or aggression is rendered safe for him. We can speculate that, in addition to providing a mask of invisibility in the clinical material described, stupidity may serve to provide a means of striking back safely at the authority or parent. Alan's behavior was in many ways destructive of his parent's and therapist's interests. He thwarted, infuriated and frustrated them. In addition to protecting him from remembering his pseudostupidity, it enabled him to effectively hurt people and not be held responsible—*after all he was sick.* In Joan's case, her disinclination to find out whether she could have a healthy child is a very poignant and devastating blow to her mother. Significantly, neither she nor her siblings want to have children of their own, and they are all depriving the mother of the sight and knowledge of grandchildren. In Joan's transference, we might also suggest that a significant amount of Joan's resistance has taken this aggressive form. Both her surfaceness and the duration of her treatment have caused the writers to speculate about a possible negative therapeutic reaction. In an important sense, perhaps these resistances have been mobilized by the hostile and aggressive aspect of the wish not to know.

Looking somewhat further afield, we can take note of several salient examples of this "function of stupidity" in the socio-cultural sphere. In pre-war Berlin, even after Hitler's assumption of the Chancellorship and Presidency in 1932, there existed a very vocal and active Cabaret. Recollections of some of the routines then current in this Cabaret are remarkable, in that political critiques and parodies were tolerated by the Nazi censors. This seeming paradox of almost seditious criticism flourishing in a totalitarian regime is explained by the feeling that the critics were regarded as "degenerate lunatics who are harmless—a diversion."

In our own recent cultural history we may recall the social critic and comedian Lenny Bruce. His acerbic commentaries on every phase of the establishment were certainly defamatory if not slanderous. Despite this, for a long period of time, because of his "insanity" he was tolerated and, in some quarters, even relished by the very establishment he vilified. Both his own aggressiveness (through humor) and the incipient potential aggressiveness of his audience, found expression and tolerance through the mask of invisibility of his "drug-induced madness."

An issue currently commanding great attention in the popular press as well as in professional, legal and mental health quarters is the complex issue of legal insanity as a defense. Brought dramatically to a head by John Hinckley Jr.'s attempted assassination of President Reagan and his adjudication as "legally insane", the whole issue of "responsibility" is being closely examined in many quarters. Public sentiment seems clearly directed against "the legal insanity verdict" and many an angry letter has been published in the newspapers decrying this brand of "copout." Perhaps in this era of ubiquitous anxiety and "angst" it is too subtle a position for society any longer to accept the validity of Ivan's thesis that "a fool cannot be blamed for his actions." Or a madman, we add.

In this paper we have reviewed the literature pertaining to the blockage and contamination of the cognitive ego function of knowledge, acquisition and processing. Two clinical examples of this process have been discussed. We have also suggested that the historical observation of the fool-truth-teller provides a somewhat different and more affirmative purpose for the adoption of this symptom. It allows for the expression with impunity, of aggressive and vengeful feelings which would not be tolerated by the person unless he put on the fool's cap. One might say that, with the assumption of pseudo-stupidity, the unconscious has parsimoniously and effectively created the conditions necessary for the individual's safe expulsion of communication of hostile, aggressive drives. The tragedy of the condition, of course, is that the price of repression is so high and that the function compromised is the very integrity of the individual's cognitive-receptive and integrative ego function.

BIBLIOGRAPHY

Abraham, K. (1913): Restriction and Transformations of Scoptophilia in Psychoneurotics. *Selected Papers.* New York: Basic Books, 1:169-234, 1955.

_____. (1924): The Influence of Oral Erotism on Character-Formation. *Selected Papers.* New York: Basic Books, 1:393-406, 1955.

Allen, D.W. (1967): Exhibitionistic and Voyeuristic Conflicts in Learning and Functioning. Psychoanal. Quart., 36:546-570.

Arlow, J.A. (1978): Pyromania and the Primal Scene: A Psychoanalytic Comment on the Work of Yukio Mishima. Psychoanal. Quart., 42:24-51.

_____. (1980): The Revenge Motive in the Primal Scene. J. Amer. Psa. Assn., 28: 519-541.

Berger, M. and Kennedy, H. (1975): Pseudobackwardness in Children: Maternal Attitudes as an Etiological Factor. *The Psychoanalytic Study of the Child.* New Haven: Yale University Press, 30:279-306.

Bergler, E. (1932): Zur Problematic der Pseudo-debilität (The Problem of Pseudodebility). Int. Ztschr. f. Psa., 16:378-399.

Blanchard, P. (1946): Psychoanalytic Contributions to the Problem of Reading Disabilities. *The Psychoanalytic Study of the Child.* New York: International Universities Press, 2:163-187.

Blum, E. (1926): The Psychology of Study and Examinations. Int. J. Psychoanal., 7:457-469.

Blum, H.P. (1974): The Borderline Childhood of the Wolf-Man. J. Amer. Psa. Assn., 22: 721-742.

_____. (1979): On the Concept and Consequences of the Primal Scene. Psychoanal. Quart., 48:27-47.

Bornstein, B. (1930): Zur Psychogenese der Pseudodebilität. (Psychogenesis of Pseudodebility) Int. Ztschr. f. Psa., 16:378-399.

Buxbaum, E. (1964): The Parents Role in the Etiology of Learning Disabilities. *The Psychoanalytic Study of the Child.* New York: International Universities Press, 19:421-477.

Esman, A.H. (1973): The Primal Scene: A Review and a Reconsideration. *The Psychoanalytic Study of the Child.* New Haven: Yale University Press, 28:49-81.

Fenichel, O. (1937): The Scoptophilic Instinct and Identification. *The Collected Papers of Otto Fenichel.* New York: W.W. Norton & Co., 1:373-397, 1953.

_____. (1945): *The Psychoanalytic Theory of Neuroses.* New York: W.W. Norton & Co.

Freud, A. (1967): Comments on Psychic Trauma. In: *Psychic Trauma.* Edited by S. Furst. New York: Basic Books, pp. 235-245.

_____. (1975): Foreword to M. Berger and H. Kennedy, Pseudobackwardness in Children. *The Psychoanalytic Study of the Child.* New Haven: Yale University Press, 30:279-306.

Freud, S. (1910): Psychogenic Visual Disturbance According to Psychoanalytic Conception. *Collected Papers.* New York: Basic Books, 2:105-112, 1959.

_____. (1918): From the History of an Infantile Neurosis. *Collected Papers.* New York: Basic Books, 3:473-605, 1959.

Glover, E. (1925): Notes on Oral Character Formation. Int. J. Psychoanal., 12:131-154.

Hellman, I. (1954): Some Observations on Mothers of Children with Intellectual Inhibitions. *The Psychoanalytic Study of the Child.* New York: International Universities Press, 9:259-273.

Herman, J.L. and Lane, R.C. (1979): Cognitive Ego Psychology and the Psychotherapy of Learning Disorders. In: *The Treatment of the Emotionally Disturbed Child.* Edited by D.S. Milman and G.D. Goldman. New York: Kendall-Hunt (to be published).

Isay, R.A. (1975): The Influence of the Primal Scene on the Sexual Behavior of an Early Adolescent. J. Amer. Psa. Assn., 23:535-553.

_____.(1978): Reporter: Panel on the Pathogenicity of the Primal Scene. J. Amer. Psa. Assn., 26:131-142.

Jacobs, T.J. (1980): Secrets, Alliances, and Family Fictions: Some Psychoanalytic Observations. J. Amer. Psa. Assn., 28:21-42.

Jarvis, V. (1958): Clinical Observations on the Visual Problem in Reading Disability. *The Psychoanalytic Study of the Child.* New York: International Universities Press, 13:451-470.

Jones, E. (1910): Simulated Foolishness in Hysteria. *Papers on Psychoanalysis.* London: Balliere, Tindall and Cox, 1st. ed., 141-153.

_____. (1949): Hamlet's Place in Mythology. In: Hamlet and Oedipus. New York: Doubleday-Anchor Press, 146-171.

Kaye, S. (1982): Psychoanalytic Perspectives on Learning Disability. J. Contemp. Psychother., 13:83-93.

Kestenberg, J. (1972): How Children Remember and Parents Forget. Int. J. Psychoanal. Psychother., 1:103-123.

Klein, E. (1949): Psychoanalytic Aspects of School Problems. *The Psychoanalytic Study of the Child.* New York: International Universities Press, 3/4:369-390.

Klein, M. (1931): A Contribution to the Theory of Intellectual Inhibition. In: *Love, Guilt and Reparation.* New York: Delacorte Press/Seymour Lawrence, 236-247, 1945.

Kris Study Group (1969): Primal Scene, Wangh Section. Plenary Presentation at the New York Psychoanalytic Institute, April 15. Unpublished.

Landauer, K. (1929): Zur Psychosexuellen Genese Der Dummheit. (On the Psychological Genesis of Stupidity). Ztschr. f. Sexualwissenschaft u. Sexualpolitik, 16:12-22.

Laufer, M. (1976): The Central Masturbation Fantasy, the Final Sexual Organization and Adolescence. *The Psychoanalytic Study of the Child.* New Haven: Yale University Press, 30:297-315.

Mahler, M.S. (1942): Pseudo-Imbecility: A Magic Cap of Invisibility. *The Selected Papers of Margaret S. Mahler.* New York: Jason Aronson, 1:3-16, 1979.

Myer, W.A. (1973): Split Self-Representation and the Primal Scene. Psychoanal. Quart., 42:525-538.

_____. (1979): Clinical Consequences of Chronic Primal Scene Exposure. Psychoanal. Quart., 48:1-25.

Oberndorf, C.P. (1939): The Feeling of Stupidity. Int. J. Psychoanal., 20:443-451.

Pearson, G.H.L. (1952): A Survey of Learning Difficulties in Children. *The Psychoanalytic Study of the Child.* New York: International Universities Press, 7:322-386.

Schmideberg, M. (1938): Intellectual Inhibition and Disturbances in Eating. Int. J. Psychoanal., 19:17-22.

Sprince, M.P. (1967): The Psychoanalytic Handling of Pseudo-Stupidity and Grossly Abnormal Behavior in a Highly Intelligent Boy. In: *The Child Analyst at Work.* Edited by E.R. Geleerd. New York: International Universities Press, 85-114.

Staver, J. (1953): The Child's Learning Difficulty as Related to the Emotional Problems of the Mother. Amer. J. Orthopsychiat., 23:131-141.
Strachey, J. (1930): Some Unconscious Factors in Reading. Int. J. Psychoanal., 11:322-331.

A Psychoanalyst's
"First Sample of the Technique"
to Work Through Inhibitions

Judith Felton

In 1937, Freud wrote:

> Obviously we cannot demand . . . that only persons of such high and rare perfection should enter the profession. But where and how is the poor wretch to acquire the ideal qualifications which he will need in his profession? The answer is, in an analysis of himself, with which . . . preparation for . . . future activity begins.

According to Freud (1937), the psychoanalyst's personal analysis has accomplished its purpose if it gives

> the learner a firm conviction of the existence of the unconscious, if it enables him, when repressed material emerges, to perceive in himself things which would otherwise be incredible to him, and if it shows him a first sample of the technique which has proved to be the only effective one in analytic work.

Despite this stance that all psychoanalysts require personal psychoanalysis for self knowledge and to work through repressions and inhibitions—which the profession has promulgated without reservation—it is rare that a psychoanalyst will discuss her or his venture in obtaining what Freud terms "a first sample of the technique." In fact, few analysts have been comfortable with this kind of sharing. This may in part be a defense against anticipated criticism of one's vulnerabilities by colleagues. It may also be a protection against expected interpretation of one's narcissistic or exhibitionistic problems. Nevertheless, whether these speculations are true or not, the most well-known exceptions to the paucity of the revelation of personal vulnerabilities have been Freud (1900), Theodor Reik (1948), and Dr. Harold Searles (1979). This situation, and also a recent presentation at a Symposium on "Inhibitions in Work, Love, and Creativity" (Felton, 1983), in which this author was requested to share a personal psychoanalytic experience, have prompted the writing of this paper.

Twenty years ago I consulted my first psychoanalyst, knowing nothing about the person, the process, or the difference between a psychiatrist, psychologist, social worker, or psychoanalyst. All I knew was that I was unhappy with my life, and that there was no one who understood me, least of all myself. I did not know what depression was, nor that I happened to be in the midst of one; and I did not know that inhibitions were conflicts which restrained one from free and spontaneous activity, nor that I happened to be exhibiting them.

As far as the man who faced me in that consultation room went, he was the strangest and weirdest composite of a person I had ever met. I had no interest in talking to him because he stared, and he said nothing except, "Tell me about yourself," and "What are your problems?" I could not tell him about myself because I was not brought up to talk about problems—and the biggest problem of that moment was he. And I certainly was not brought up to tell parents and professionals (authority figures, if you will) that they were my problem. All I knew was that the man opposite me was too skinny, too ugly, too unfriendly, and talked in ways I had never in my twenty years heard anyone talk. He did not seem "normal" to me. And it did not seem at all normal for me to tell him this.

Since I told my family I could not stand this man, and since my family could see that I was not getting better, they found me another psychiatrist with psychoanalytic traininig—this time someone who had a reputation (and a waiting list) for dealing with "Young People." After this man made it clear he would take me only if my parents agreed to stay out of the treatment, we made an appointment. This was someone to whom I could relate. Although the transference was most often positive, the negative emerged and was analyzed.

I found psychoanalytic psychology books in Gimbel's and reported on the three volumes of Horn-ee which I had read. With a smile and kindness, he corrected me with a nod, and said, "Horney." If I asked, timidly of course, about the book on the shelf by Fritz Redl, titled *The Aggressive Child,* he answered. Rather than interpreting, before I was ready, that I was the aggressive child who was beginning to flower, he asked if I wanted the book.

When I launched into worries about doing the right thing, and following all of the rules of etiquette with which I had been diligently brought up, he enabled me to talk about my fears and wishes. And he told me anecdotes about professors and people in very high places who did outrageously human things, which did not follow the rules of etiquette by any stretch of my imagination. I especially liked hearing about the director of the psychoanalytic institute who kept carrot sticks and celery in his file cabinet, because he, like myself, had a problem with eating too much.

Dr. "X" even said "So what?" to serious moralistic commentaries, and he proceeded to loosen my superego, build my ego, and give my id permission to breathe, as I was only just beginning to learn the definitions of these words. When I had my first dream which included him, we both knew that my analysis had begun. Only neither of us could know that the dream, in which I was hurriedly running around Pennsylvania Station to end up behind a large desk working alongside him, would eventually lead me to my work today.

He was a good psychiatrist and a typical psychoanalyst . . . he did not offer premature interpretations, nor did he pretend to be a psychic and make predictions. He simply interpreted the transference in my dream, and he understood my wishes to be with him, to be like him, and to do his work.

I experienced him as one of the wisest individuals I had ever known. To him that would be overvaluing his role and underestimating my own. I was a difficult patient. There was no way in those years he could know that he was getting much of anywhere.

For the first year in treatment I did not talk, at least not much. My symptoms got worse instead of better. I cried more, not less. I slept more, not less. I cut myself off from family and friends, and no one recognized the intelligent and successful young woman who had once been. When I started to observe my analyst' errors, there appeared to be some progress.

I now know how difficult it is to do for a patient what he did for me . . . to just sit and encourage, tell anecdotal stories to keep himself from going batty, and watch the Kleenex disappear. Then make interpretations once in a while, and wait for "her" to talk a little bit.

Why am I revealing this personal story at this time? For three reasons: First, Freud emphasizes the importance of the "first sample of the technique'' which has proved to be the only effective one in analytic work; second, to write about myself twenty years ago is less anxiety-provoking than to write about the psychoanalysis which terminated five years ago; and third, because it is my most dramatic and significant personal psychoanalytic experience. It is possibly the one from which I learned the most, not only as a patient and analysand, but also as a psychotherapist and psychoanalyst.

From these painful introductory years, I learned the benefit of sitting hour after hour with another person, watching her or him seem to get nowhere, and sometimes get worse—and of listening to frustration after frustration yet still adhering to the rules of psychoanalysis. In my experience there is no substitute for providing an environment in which the patient feels able to talk. Then one is able to allow the unconscious to become conscious by following the method of free association.

As analysts agree, the most effective way is the interpretation of the patient's thoughts and feelings about the analyst, which is the interpretation of the transference. And the most effective way to get to this is through the analysis of the obstacles and blocks that stand in the way of the person's telling what she or he really thinks and feels, which is the analysis of the resistances. Psychoanalysis and psychoanalytic psychotherapy make the obvious plain, but the method is neither obvious, nor is it plain. It is systematic and takes time to master, and it is difficult if also rewarding.

I am sharing this to illustrate my thought that a personal psychoanalytic experience is the best way to understand, from the inside out, what psychoanalysis can do, and what it cannot do. I also believe that there is no shortcut. There may be a number of ways to attempt to make the process more efficient, such as other types of therapy. There may also be a number of ways to improve the external quality of one's life, such as making more money, taking more vacations, and having a fuller love life. However, my experience is that the preferred way to assure quality in one's inner life is to work through one's inhibitions, so there is internal pleasure in love and work, and heightened capacity for both creativity and play.

At the same time, it is important to me to conclude with some sobering comments. Psychoanalysis is an aid to living, not a substitute for living. It is a rare human being who goes through life without some physical illness and bodily ailment, from which psychoanalysis does not rescue us. Sometimes no psychoanalysis is better than bad psychoanalysis—and sometimes if a person gets stomachaches only from eating mushrooms, it seems to make more sense to avoid mushrooms than to pursue a lengthy psychoanalysis. Finally, while psychoanalysis may offer us fewer inhibitions and more joy for our time here on earth, it cannot offer us perfection or eternal life, except in our most magical fantasies, whether on the couch or off.

REFERENCES

Felton, J. R. (1983). "Inhibitions and Personal Psychoanalysis—Why Bother?" Presented at the New York Center for Psychoanalytic Training Eighth Annual Symposium, April 9, 1983.
Freud, S. (1900). "The Method of Interpreting Dreams: An Analysis of a Speciman Dream," in *The Interpretation of Dreams.* Standard Edition, IV.
Freud, S. (1937). "Analysis Terminable and Interminable," Standard Edition, XXIII.
Reik, T. (1948). *Listening with the Third Ear.* New York: Farrar, Straus, and Company.
Searles, H. (1979). *Countertransference and Related Subjects.* New York: International Universities Press, Inc.

The Concept of Priming Work in Professional Creativity

Richard I. Harrison

The concept of human creativity is very broad. It has been described in different ways and from different points of view including the person, the process, the product, work, motivation, inspiration, inhibition, the family, the society, the culture, libido, aggression, and mental health. A study of the literature on creativity reveals a diversity of descriptions which suggests that creativity may be multiply determined. It follows that any singular approach to the subject may be misleading. Nevertheless, a specialized view of the creative product, creative process, and creative work will be presented which has practical relevance in a large number of cases. The focus will be on professionally oriented creativity carried out with at least some degree of intention.

The definition of creativity is assumed to be founded on the quality of the creative result. The creative quality is taken to be related to the size of the leap in novel or aesthetic quality when compared to already existing creative accomplishments. The quality of the creative result, and therefore the size of the leap, is ultimately determined by the world of peers as well as other knowledgeable people. Examples of extremely high quality creative results include Beethoven's musical contributions, Da Vinci's art and inventions, Einstein's theories of relativity, Freud's theories on psychoanalysis, and Shakespeare's plays. Examples of somewhat lower quality creative results include Berlin's songs, Edison's inventions, Twain's stories, and Whistler's paintings. It follows that an extremely high quality creative result generally astounds the peer world while lesser quality results cause smaller feelings of surprise. The implication of astonishment and surprise is that the creative individual's ego assets in certain areas either already exceeded or has been temporarily "stretched" beyond those of his peers. "Stretching" beyond one's ego assets is defined as piercing some of the experientially de-

79

termined adaptations and defenses which maintain the homoeostasis of our existing ego assets. The homoeostasis tends to preserve life but tends to impede creativity. On the other hand, a creative individual with comparatively superior ego assets can turn out creative products in a routine fashion without "stretching" his ego assets and yet his peers are astounded or surprised because these products do not seem routine to them.

It is likely that a significant proportion of creative individuals in the genius class had inborn tendencies that were then reinforced by environmental factors which propelled the development of highly advanced ego assets. It is likely that a significant proportion of creative individuals not in the genius class are relatively equivalent when it comes to creatively useful inborn tendencies and the ego assets that are subsequently developed. This paper will focus on this type of creative individual and in particular on an approach to the creative process which is likely to be of wide practical importance. This approach describes the creative process where the creative individual temporarily "stretches" his ego assets beyond that of his peers.

The discussion that follows first deals with the most prominent psychoanalytic view of the creative process which is based on the concept that creative purposes are served during a partial ego regression which allows the fantastically free styles of primary process thinking to contribute to the creative process. It is a hypothesis of this paper that these regressed ego states are, for the most part, the commonly experienced self limited ego regressions normally occurring in everyday life. A particular contribution of this paper is the contention that special mental work called priming work should take place before the ego regression occurs. The concept of priming work within the creative process is considered to be crucial in many practical forms of creativity and its description will therefore receive special emphasis in this article.

The discussion later will also deal with a second and less prominent psychoanalytic view of the creative process. This view is based on the concept that the creative advantages of some of the fantastic styles of primary process thinking can be brought into the creative process without the necessity of an ego regression occurring at all. It is hypothesized that this type of creative process produces creative products of lesser quality when compared to those products produced with an ego regression. It is also hypothesized that this type of creativity requires priming work.

Before embarking on the discussion of the creativity that does involve an ego regression, a personal creative experience will be described that is pertinent to the ideas presented in this paper. This writer, prior to becoming a psychoanalyst, was a scientific researcher, a professor in the physical sciences, and an inventor who produced a number of patents. One invention received a national citation as being among the one hundred most significant for the year in the area of specialty. Another invention was used on a space probe to measure the surface temperature of the planet Venus. This writer had a reputation among his peers of being creative. The mental processes which led to these inventions seemed, in every case, to involve some form of self limited ego regression. These ego regressions occurred mostly within day dreams. One invention was conceptualized at the end of the transition between the sleep and the awake states. Another was produced during routine, almost thoughtless activities (mowing the lawn). These experiences with inventing led to the hypothesis that creativity can involve a naturally occurring self limited partial ego regression. The contention mentioned earlier concerning priming work which produces preconscious and unconscious residues in memory was derived from an interpretation of one of this writer's dreams. The dream occurred after months of intense work reviewing the psychology of creativity. This review was motivated by the feeling that there was not enough emphasis on the importance of preparatory work. This work is called priming work in this paper.

The dream that follows is called the book machine dream. This writer was loading old books into a book making machine that was quiescent. The inner parts of the machine could be seen. The loaded books seemed to adhere only to the outer parts of the machine when the work of loading involved normal effort. The books adhered to the inner fundamental parts, as well as to the outer parts, when the loading work was extremely strenuous. The machine somehow started to function some time after the loading work was over. The machine operated in what seemed a normal way. The books processed were only those that had adhered to the outer parts. The machine produced ordinary new books using pages and parts of the aforementioned books that adhered to the outer parts. Occasionally the machine would operate in an abnormal way. This abnormal operation involved the books that adhered to the inner fundamental parts as well as those that adhered to the outer parts. This abnormal operation produced beautiful new and unusual books whose title was

Genesis. The almost obvious interpretation of the dream was that the book machine was this writer's mind. The hard work loading books which made them adhere to the inner fundamental parts corresponded to the concept of intense priming work which produces unconscious and preconscious residues of memory traces. The abnormal operation involving the books adhering to both the inner fundamental parts and to the outer parts corresponds to a self limited ego regression where the residues of memory traces produced by priming work are processed by the fantastic styles characteristic of primary process thinking. The beautiful new books called *Genesis* correspond to a trial creative outcome. Note that the hypothesis suggested by the dream is verified by the very process that produced the dream!

The creative process will be modeled by four consecutive distinct phases. Briefly these phases are: the initial motivation phase, the priming work phase, the ego regression phase, and the elaboration and assessment phase. Practically, the phases do not have distinct boundaries and often merge with each other. Nevertheless the model will be used since it greatly simplifies the task of presentation. The second phase, which discusses the concept of priming work, will be emphasized since it is a key contribution in this paper.

The first phase involves an occurrence which provides the initial motivation for the creative process and defines the creative aim. This phase is called the initial motivation phase. The initial motivation can be provided in several ways. One way is by the demands made by others. An example of such an initial motivation is that of an artist who received a commission to produce a painting. This led to a creative work of note. Another example is of a scientist who received a grant to find a vaccine. He ultimately found the vaccine and recognition for being creative. The initial motivation can also come from the creative individual's conscious external observations. One example is that of an artist who was emotionally moved by the sights of starving children in his travels in Africa. He felt motivated to paint this theme of starving children. One such painting is currently being considered for use in a publication on world hunger.

The initial motivation can come from an eruption to consciousness of formerly unconscious memories. These eruptions may take place within dreams, day dreams, fantasies, free associations, and other ego states where the defenses guarding the unconscious are lowered. An example of such an initial motivation was reported during therapy. An artist told of a visit to his aged aunt. During the visit he found himself day dreaming and had a vision of a very festive scene which he associated to childhood. The vision was described to his aunt, who said it seemed to be the scene of his mother's wedding. The artist's mother had remarried when he was almost three years old. The artist had not attended the wedding and to his knowledge had never heard it described. The vision motivated him to paint scenes of weddings, one of which won him artistic acclaim.

The second phase is called the priming work phase. Priming work is guided and motivated by the wish to create as determined in the first phase. It consists of a consciously focused and often intense study of already known, as well as newly acquired, knowledge, theories, techniques, themes, compositions, styles, and existing creative products, all of which have been judged to be relevant to the creative aim. Priming work produces and adds relatively strong preconscious and unconscious memory trace constellations of relevant intellectual or emotional subject matter to the total memory. The emotional subject matter includes a strong wish to fulfill the creative aim. During and after the priming work phase, there is a tendency for the aforementioned memory trace constellations to remain relatively strong. This raises the probability that these constellations will be the ones processed during the ensuing self limited partial ego regression, which will be discussed later.

There is another tendency which is evident during and after the priming work phase. The strong wish to create, which is included in the memory trace constellations produced by priming work, stimulates an increase to occur in the frequency or number of self limited ego regressions over that which would take place naturally. Other interesting manifestations seem to result from priming work. One example was provided by a writer during therapy. A humorous news report produced an urge in him to write a situation comedy based on the story. He carried out intensive studies of comedies and comedy bits which seemed to relate to the flavor of the news story. He gave numerous accounts in therapy of incidents where parts of his studies would spontaneously "pop" into conscious awareness while he was engaged in non-creative or non-humorous tasks. It therefore can be concluded that the subject matter of priming work may spontaneously erupt into conscious awareness at times when there is no demand for this awareness.

Another manifestation of priming work was evident in this

writer's experience as well as in the experience of some of his patients. Priming work seems to produce an unusually high sense of expertise in the individual. There seems to be an intellectual or emotional understanding of detailed depths along with a global view of the creatively relevant subject matter. This unusual level of understanding lasts for some time after priming work ends. An example of this manifestation was provided by a scientist during therapy. After intense studies of certain topics in physics, he was able to visualize every detailed step in a complicated atomic problem in quantum mechanics and simultaneously visualize practical applications in the world of large objects that are billions upon billions of times larger than atoms. These simultaneous theoretical microscopic and practical macroscopic views were not ordinarily available to him in his professional thinking. He described this as a sense of expertise which lasted about three months after the intense studies ended.

The priming work described thus far might more accurately be called intentional priming work. This leaves room for contributions to the hierarchy of preconscious and unconscious memory trace constellations which were not guided by the specific creative aim of the first phase. This type of mental activity might be classed as unintentional priming work. Unintentional priming work includes the prior work done in developing professional competence, background, and skills also used in the creative process. Hereafter, priming work will include the concepts of intentional and unintentional priming work.

The third phase is called the ego regression phase, in which the ego is "stretched" in a metaphorical sense. During the ego regression, critical mental processes take place which serve the creative aim. The phase terminates when the regression ends and a conscious trial creative outcome is produced. A trial creative outcome must be tested before it can be determined if it is a creative product, as will be discussed in the next phase.

The regressive state during creativity has been experienced in many ways. One such regressive experience was presented earlier as the book machine dream. Another experience was provided by a creative engineer. He reported that he was aware of highly accelerated, childlike, and erratic thinking which seemed to violate some scientific rules but kept others during the creative process. The accelerated thinking suddenly stopped and produced a trial creative outcome which ultimately proved to be a creative product.

This writer's experience in inventing in the physical sciences indicates that the regressive experience can occur during the awake state while the mind is engaged in routine concerns. One experience occurred while he was a passenger in a car and watching the various roadside features go by. Suddenly, there was a sense that his mind was "rushing" or thinking without total conscious awareness. The "rushing" terminated and a physical idea sprang into consciousness. It proved to be the core of an invention which fulfilled some current scientific needs. The idea was patented, gained recognition, and put to practical use.

A survey of this writers' experiences, his patients' experiences, and the reported experiences of creative people leads to the observation that creative experiences can be manifest in many ways. These include dreams, day dreams, fantasies, free associations, transitions from sleep to awake states, transitions from awake states to sleep states, and during awake states when the mind is engaged in highly routine mental activities. This leads to the conclusion that the ego was, in each case, partially regressed for limited periods of time, after which a trial creative outcome was suddenly produced. The regressive mental activity has been described as aesthetic selection, creative hunches, playing, artistic experimentation, creative imagination, innovative exploration, scientific speculation, educated guesses, and intuitive choices. The sudden production of a trial creative outcome has been labeled as an "aha" experience, an illumination experience, and a sudden vision.

Theoretically, the ego regression phase can be explained as follows. There are two possible inputs from the total stored memory that fuels the ego regression phase. The first input consists of the preconscious and unconscious memory trace constellations that were directly inserted by priming work. The second input consists of certain non-primed preconscious and unconscious memories primitively associated to the primed memories. The primitive associations are dynamically part of and take place during regressive primary process thinking. The first and second inputs, regardless of their source or manner of associative selection, are even further processed by the primitive styles of primary process thinking. The primitive styles of primary process thinking are often evident in dreams and have fantastic qualities. These styles include loose non-reality guided associations, disassociations, concretizations, organizations, condensations, displacements, reversals, superpositions, substitutions, and symbolizations.

The theoretical concept of ego regression in creativity was called regression in the service of the ego as first proposed by Kris (1952) and elaborated by Kubie (1958) and others. Their collective work suggested that primary process thinking is utilized in creativity and occurs during a temporary, controlled, adaptive, partial ego regression. It is hypothesized in this paper that the creative ego regression is predominantly a common, naturally occurring, regressive ego state which is self limited in depth and duration. These ego states tend to serve the creative purpose when the preceding priming work is strong enough. Otherwise these naturally occurring self limited ego regressions serve other purposes. The theoretical premise of naturally occurring ego regressions in the creative process is supported by the book machine dream and creative experiences reported in the literature and by patients.

The fourth phase is called the elaboration and assessment phase. During this phase the trial creative outcome produced in the prior phase may be elaborated and expanded by the application of ordinary competent secondary process thinking. Regressive styles of thinking are not involved in any way. For example, a mathematician might convert his trial creative outcome which, in this case, is a proposed theorem, from an algebraic form into a geometric form. Or an artist will make background additions to the trial creative figures in his painting. The elaborated trial creative outcome is then assessed by the creative individual from the point of view of reality acceptance and novel or aesthetic qualities. The assessment of reality acceptance implies that the trial creative outcome will be accepted by the world as a real contribution to the quality of human life. The assessment that the trial creative outcome will be seen as a leap in novel or aesthetic accomplishments would lead the creative person to the conclusion that he has produced a creative product. If the trial creative outcome is assessed as a creative product by the creative individual, it is then communicated to the world for peer assessment. If the trial creative outcome is assessed as not fulfilling the requirements for a creative product, the second phase or the second and third phases may be started again in order to produce another trial creative outcome.

The focus of this paper will now turn toward creativity where there is no ego regression. This creative process will also be described by a sequence of four phases. The first phase is called the initial motivation phase and is identical to the initial motivation phase discussed before. The second phase is called the priming work phase and is also identical to the priming work discussed before. The third phase is called the non-regressive styles of thinking phase. Bush (1969) and Suler (1980) proposed that a creative individual can consciously apply some of the styles of primary process thinking in the creative process without the necessity of any ego regression. This is accomplished by developing some exceptional ego assets prior to the creative activity. These exceptional ego assets arise from the incorporation of many styles of primary process thinking into the repertory of secondary process thought. Any competent psychoanalyst, for example, must have incorporated many styles of primary process thinking into the repertory of his secondary process thought. It is just this incorporation that allows him to translate the manifest content of dreams, fantasies, and other session contents into more analytically useful latent meanings.

The application of the incorporated styles of primary process thought to the strong preconscious and unconscious memory trace constellations from the priming work phase produces a trial creative outcome similar to the earlier discussed case where there is an ego regression. However there are important differences when comparing this third phase to the prior third phase involving an ego regression. One difference is that there are no contributions to the trial creative outcome from unconscious memories. A second difference is that there tends to be less looseness or fantastic qualities in the application of the incorporated styles of primary process thinking.

It is hypothesized here that these differences result in trial creative outcomes of lesser quality when there is no ego regression involved. Certain types of art are likely to be excluded by this type of non-regressive creative process because the emergence of repressed unconscious memories is fundamental to some artistic creativity. it is likely, on the other hand, that creative problem solving does often involve the type of creativity in which the styles of primary process thinking are incorporated into secondary process thought.

The fourth and last phase of the sequence is called the elaboration and assessment phase. It is identical to the elaboration and assessment phase discussed earlier.

This article has now been completed in so far as the main contention and hypotheses are concerned. This writer found that the experience of writing this paper was in itself priming work. This was evident during a taxi ride when a sudden illumination occurred. The illumination seemed to connect psychoanalytic therapy with creativity in the following way. Priming work in creativity is, in part, analogous to working through in treatment. In working through, the patient experiences a number of interventions which repetitively brings a targeted pathological dynamic into conscious awareness. This work also places these experiences into a strong position in the hierarchy of preconsciousness and unconsciousness. When these memory traces are strong enough and when the resistance to the therapeutic change weakens, it is possible that "corrective" ego regressions take place. These regressions might serve to change the hierarchy of memory still further so as to neutralize or compensate for the memories that supported pathological mental conflict.

REFERENCES USED IN THE PAPER
AND IN THE PRIMING WORK

Bellak, L. Creativity: Some random notes to a systematic consideration. *Journal of Projective Techniques,* 1958, 22, 363-380.

Bellak, L. Toward systematic consideration of the nature of the genesis of the creative process. In D. P. Spence (Ed.), *The Broad Scope of Psychoanalysis.* New York: Grune and Stratton, 1967.

Bush, M. Psychoanalysis and scientific creativity. *Journal of the American Psychoanalytic Association,* 1969, 17, 136-191.

Corbin, E. I. The autonomous ego functions in creativity. *Journal of the American Psychoanalytic Association,* 1974, 22, 568-587.

Ehrenzweig, A. Unconscious mental images in art and science. *Nature,* 1962, 194, 1008-1012.

Fine, R. Work, depression and creativity. *Psychological Reports,* 1980, 46, 1195-1221.

Giovacchini, P. I. On scientific creativity. *Journal of the American Psychoanalytic Association,* 1960, 8, 407-426.

Giovacchini, P. I. Characterological features in the creative personality. *Journal of the American Psychoanalytic Association,* 1971, 19, 524-542.

Greenacre, P. *Emotional Growth.* New York: International Universities Press, 1971.

Kris, E. *Psychoanalytic Explorations in Art.* New York: International Universities Press, 1952.

Kubie, L. S. *Neurotic Distortions of the Creative Process.* New York: Noonday Press, 1958.

Scachtel, E. G. *Metamorphosis.* New York: Basic Books, 1959.

Suler, J. R. Primary process thinking and creativity. *Psychological Bulletin,* 1980, 88, 144-165.